KB269994

영어 독해력 증강 프로그램

행복한 명작 읽기 **48**

주홍글씨

The Scarlet Letter

다락원

행복한 명작 읽기

　어린 시절 누구나 한번쯤 읽게 되는 아름다운 동화와 명작들은 훗날 어른이 되어서도 따뜻한 기억으로 가슴에 남기 마련이죠. 이제 영어로 다시 한번 명작의 세계에 빠져 보는 건 어떨까요? 한글 번역본에서는 절대 느낄 수 없는 원작의 깊이를 그 느낌 그대로 맛볼 수 있고, 이미 알고 있는 이야기들이라 어렵지 않습니다. 즐겁게 읽어 나가는 사이에 독해력이 쑥쑥 자라는 것은 기본이죠.

　「행복한 명작 읽기」 시리즈는 기초가 약한 영어 초급자나 초, 중, 고등 학생들이 보다 즐겁고 효과적으로 영어 명작들을 읽으며 독해력을 키울 수 있도록 개발된 독해력 증강 프로그램입니다.

　초보자를 위한 250단어 수준에서 중고급자를 위한 1,000단어 수준까지 6단계로 구성되어 있는 이 프로그램은 단계별로 효과적인 영어 읽기 요령을 제시하고 영문 고유의 참맛을 느낄 수 있는 장치를 곳곳에 마련하고 있습니다. 영어표현 및 문법에 대한 친절한 설명, 어휘 학습과 내용의 이해를 돕는 퀴즈들, 그리고 매 페이지 펼쳐지는 멋진 그림들까지 어디 한 군데 소홀함 없이 구성했습니다. 여기에 권말 특별부록 '리스닝 길잡이'를 곁들여 읽기에서 그치지 않고 체계적인 듣기 학습까지 아우르고 있습니다. 또한 CD에 '오디오북' 형식으로 전문 미국 성우들의 생동감 넘치는 원음을 담았습니다.

　본문은 단계별 독자들의 수준을 고려하여 원어민 전문 필진이 교육부 선정 어휘를 가지고 표준 미국식 영어로 리라이팅하였기 때문에 정규 교과 학습에도 큰 도움이 될 것입니다. 「행복한 명작 읽기」를 통해 영어를 읽고 듣는 재미에 푹 빠져 보시기 바랍니다.

행복한 명작 읽기 연구회

Introduction

나다니엘 호손

Nathaniel Hawthorne

(1804 ~ 1864)

미국의 소설가. 매우 엄격한 청교도 집안에서 자란 호손은 어릴 때부터 책 읽기를 좋아했다. 대학 졸업 후 고향에서 잡지에 글을 기고하면서 문필생활을 시작한 그는, 1837년 첫 소설을 발표하여 문인으로서 인정받기 시작했고 1850년에 《주홍글씨》를 내놓았다.

호손은 인간의 죄의식과 내적 문제에 관심을 갖고, 죄악, 양심 등의 문제를 탐구하는 데 노력을 기울인 작가로 알려져 있다. 특히 그는 자신의 성장배경인 청교도주의의 전통을 계승하여 도덕적·종교적 죄악에 빠진 사람들, 자기중심적 고독에 사로잡힌 사람들의 내면을 도덕·종교·심리의 세 가지 측면에서 엄밀히 묘사하였다.

《주홍글씨》 이외에 그의 작품으로는 《낡은 목사관의 이끼》(1846), 《일곱 박공의 집》(1851), 《블라이드데일 로맨스》(1852), 《탱글우드 이야기》(1853), 《대리석의 목양신》(1860) 등이 있다.

「주홍글씨」는 17세기 중엽 보스턴의 청교도 식민지를 배경으로 하여, 간통 사건을 둘러싼 세 사람(헤스터 프린, 아서 딤스데일, 로저 칠링워스)의 삼각관계를 바탕으로, 엄격하고 가혹한 청교도 사회의 인습적 도덕과 제재, 그 속에서 고통 받는 주인공들의 슬픔과 고독, 회한 등을 그린 작품이다.

남편보다 먼저 미국에 건너와 살던 헤스터 프린은 간통으로 펄이라는 여자아이를 낳고, 그 죄로 인해 주홍글씨 A자를 평생 가슴에 달고 살아야 하는 형벌을 선고받는다. 그러나 그녀는 간통한 상대가 누구인지는 결코 밝히지 않는다. 오랜 세월 행방불명이었던 그녀의 남편 칠링워스는 그녀가 공개 처벌을 받던 날 헤스터 앞에 나타난 후, 자기 신분을 숨기고 의사로서 행세하며 그 상대를 찾아 복수하기로 결심한다. 한편, 헤스터의 간통 상대인 젊은 딤스데일 목사는 양심의 가책으로 인해 스스로를 괴롭히며 엄격한 고행을 하다 건강이 점점 악화되는데…

contents

The Scarlet Letter

주홍글씨

Before You Read

Hester Prynne 헤스터 프린

I am a beautiful and independent woman, but my life is miserable and unlucky. I am married woman, but I had an affair with another man and had a baby. Now the townspeople want me to tell them who the father of my child is! However, I will never tell. I will never betray another person.

난 아름답고 독립심 강한 여성이죠. 하지만 내 삶은 비참하고 불행해요. 난 결혼한 여자인데, 다른 남자와 간통을 해서 아이를 낳았어요. 이제 마을 사람들은 내 아이의 아버지가 누군지 내가 말하길 바라죠. 하지만 절대 얘기하지 않을 거예요. 또 한 사람을 배신하진 않겠어요.

independent 독립심이 강한 **miserable** 비참한, 불쌍한 **affair** 연애 사건, 정사 **betray** 배반하다

Reverend Dimmesdale 딤스데일 목사

Oh, my life is wretched! I tell people to behave properly, and to live according to God's will. They respect me despite my youth. Yet, I am not worthy of their respect. I have a terrible secret that is burned upon the skin above my heart. Oh, how can I wash away my guilt and be free once more?

아, 내 인생은 비참해! 난 사람들에게 올바로 처신하고 신의 뜻에 따라 살라고 말한다오. 그들은 내가 젊은데도 날 존경하지. 하지만 난 그들의 존경을 받을 가치가 없어. 나에겐 심장 위 피부에서 불타는 끔찍한 비밀이 있거든. 아, 어떻게 하면 내 죄를 씻어 버리고 다시 한번 자유로워질 수 있을까?

reverend 목사 **wretched** 비참한 **behave properly** 올바로 행동하다 **respect** 존경하다; 존경 **be worthy of** ~의 가치가 있다 **guilt** 죄가 있음

Pearl 펄

While other children have a father, I don't! However, this does not bother me too much. I am free to play and do what I want most of the time. The adults think that I have no manners, but they are all too serious and boring for me!

다른 아이들은 아버지가 있는데 난 없지요. 하지만 그런 건 별로 신경 쓰이지 않아요. 난 거의 늘 내 맘대로 놀고 내가 하고 싶은 대로 하죠. 어른들은 내가 예의 없다고 생각하지만, 내가 보기엔 어른들은 전부 다 너무 진지하고 지루해요!

bother 괴롭히다, 귀찮게 하다 **adult** 어른 **manners** 예의범절 **serious** 진지한, 심각한 **boring** 지루한

Roger Chillingworth 로저 칠링워스

When I was away, my wife had a baby with another man. But I did not blame her. She always told me that she did not love me. However, I do blame the father of the baby. I will find out who he is and punish him for his cowardly silence.

내가 멀리 떠나 있을 때, 내 아내는 다른 남자의 아이를 낳았어. 하지만 난 그녀를 탓하지 않았소. 그녀는 날 사랑하지 않는다고 늘 말했으니까. 하지만 난 아기의 아빠는 비난하오. 그가 누군지 알아내서 비겁하게 침묵하는 그를 벌하겠어.

blame 나무라다, 비난하다 **find out** 알아내다 **cowardly** 비겁한 **silence** 침묵, 잠잠함

Pastor John Wilson & Governor Bellingham 존 윌슨 목사 & 벨링햄 주지사

It is our duty to make sure our Puritan society lives according to the will of God. Hester Pyrnne must reveal to us who the father of her child is. Only then will she be forgiven by God.

우리의 청교도 사회가 반드시 하나님의 뜻에 따라 살도록 하는 것이 우리의 의무요. 헤스터 프린은 아이의 아버지가 누구인지 반드시 밝혀야만 하오. 그렇게 해야만 하나님에게 용서받을 것이오.

duty 임무, 일 **make sure** 꼭 ~하다, 확인하다 **will** 의지, 뜻 **forgive** 용서하다

CHAPTER ONE

A Terrible Sin

Although the forefathers of the Boston Colony strove to create a utopian society, two of the first things they built when they made their town were a cemetery and a prison.[1] On this day, twenty years after the first Puritan settlers arrived in the New World colony, the townspeople gathered outside the prison.

"Good women," proclaimed one woman, "if we judged wicked women like Hester Prynne, she would not have the easy sentence that the town magistrates have handed her!"[2]

- sin (종교상 · 도덕상의) 죄, 죄악
- forefather 조상, 선조
- colony 식민지
- strive to부정사 ~하려고 노력하다
  (strive-strove-striven)
- utopian 이상향의, 유토피아의
- cemetery 공동묘지
- Puritan 청교도; 청교도의
- settler 이주자, 개척자, 식민자
- proclaim 공연히 비난하다; 선언하다

- judge 재판하다, 판결하다
- wicked 사악한, 부도덕한
- sentence 선고, 판결; 선고하다
- magistrate 행정장관, 치안판사
- brand (죄인 등에) 소인을 찍다
- place 두다, 놓다
- spike 대못, 담장못
- figure (사람의) 모습, 형상
- usher 안내하다, 인도하다
- step out 걸어 나오다

"Yes!" agreed another woman. "They should at least brand the mark upon her forehead with a hot iron! By placing the mark on the front of her gown, she can cover it up anytime!"

"Yes!" cried another, "She may cover it as she likes, but the mark will always be on her heart!"

Then the prison door, covered in iron spikes, flew open. A large, frightening figure in black came out from the inner darkness. With his hand, he tried to usher out a young woman. But she pushed the hand away and stepped out into the open by her own free will, with an air of dignity.[3]

1 보스턴 식민지의 선조들은 이상적인 사회를 만들어 내기 위해 노력했지만, 그들이 마을을 만들 때 처음 세운 것 중 두 가지가 바로 묘지와 감옥이었다.

2 우리가 헤스터 프린 같은 부도덕한 여인들을 심판한다면, 그녀는 마을 치안판사들이 그녀에게 내린 그런 가벼운 형량을 선고 받진 않을 거예요! → 가정법 과거

3 그러나 그녀는 그 손을 뿌리치고 근엄한 태도로 자진해서 광장으로 걸어 나왔다.
→ by one's own free will: 자신의 자유 의지로 / an air of dignity: 근엄한 태도

In the woman's arms was a three-month-old baby. The baby winked because it was the first time it had ever felt sunlight on its face. The mother, standing fully revealed amid the townspeople, lowered the baby in her arm to show her gown.[1] She was blushing, but she wore a proud smile. On the breast of her gown was a large letter A. The letter was made of fine, red cloth and embroidered with rich, gold thread. The design was artistic and fanciful.

Hester Prynne was a tall young woman, with an elegant figure and dark gleaming hair. Those who knew her were amazed at her beauty and ladylike comportment under these circumstances.[2]

"She certainly has great skill with the sewing needle," remarked one of the women, "but what a shameful way to show it!"

□ wink 눈을 깜빡거리다	□ fanciful 환상적인, 기발한
□ reveal 드러내다	□ elegant 우아한
□ lower 내리다	□ gleam 빛나다
□ blush 얼굴을 붉히다	□ comportment 처신, 태도, 행동
□ breast 가슴	□ circumstances 〈복수형〉 상황, 환경
□ embroider 수를 놓다	□ sewing needle 바늘
□ thread 실	□ remark 말하다
□ artistic 예술적인; 정교한	□ shameful 부끄러운, 창피스러운

1 마을 사람들 한가운데 완전히 모습을 드러내고 서 있는 그 어머니는 드레스를 보여 주기 위해 팔에 안긴 아기를 밑으로 내렸다. → amid: ~의 한복판에

"Make way in the King's name!" shouted the prison officer. "Everyone will have a chance to get a good view of this wicked woman from now until noon.[3] Come along, Hester. Show your scarlet letter in the marketplace!"

✔ *Check Up*

Check the best description of how Hester Prynne accepted her punishment.

a With sorrow
b With defiance
c With shame

정답 : q

2 그녀를 아는 사람들은 그녀의 아름다움과 이런 상황 속에서도 기품 있는 태도에 깜짝 놀랐다.
   → be amazed at: ~에 깜짝 놀라다

3 모든 사람들은 지금부터 정오까지 이 부도덕한 여인을 잘 볼 수 있는 기회를 가질 거요.
   → get a view of: ~을 보다

A lane opened up between the spectators, and Hester Prynne walked toward the area appointed for public punishment. Calmly, she came to the scaffold at the western end of the marketplace, next to Boston's oldest church. The scaffold was a platform where punishments were carried out publicly so as to impress the citizenry into obeying the laws.[1]

There was a pillory there, designed to hold a human head tightly and keep it in the public gaze. But Hester Prynne was not sentenced to its confinement. Her sentence was just to stand on the platform for three hours.

☐ lane 통로; 좁은 길	☐ confinement 감금, 유폐
☐ spectator 구경꾼	☐ onlooker 방관자, 구경꾼
☐ appointed 정해진, 지정된	☐ solemn 엄숙한, 근엄한
☐ scaffold 단두대, 처형대	☐ assault 습격; 격한 공격, 비난
☐ platform 대, 연단; 플랫폼	☐ scorn 경멸, 조롱
☐ carry out 실행하다	☐ insult 모욕
☐ impress 명심시키다; ~에게 깊은 인상을 주다	☐ surface 떠오르다, 부상하다; 표면
☐ the citizenry 일반 시민	☐ glow 빛, 작열
☐ obey 복종하다	☐ dim 흐릿한, 희미한
☐ pillory 칼(목과 손을 널빤지 사이에 끼우는 형틀)	☐ pale 창백한
☐ gaze 응시; 응시하다	☐ cloistered 세상을 등진
☐ be sentenced to ~을 선고 받다	☐ misshapen 보기 흉한, 기형의

She climbed the steps and began her sentence. The onlookers stared at her and the scarlet letter in solemn silence. Hester had prepared herself to face the assault of the public's scorn and insults, but she found their heavy silence almost more difficult to bear.[2] When she stood there, her mind began to travel back into itself as memories began to surface.[3] She could see and feel the days of her happy childhood. Then she saw her face, gazing in the mirror, and its glow of young beauty. Then she saw the face of a man who was much older. His eyes were dim, and his skin was pale from many years of cloistered study. His figure was slightly misshapen, his left shoulder a bit higher than his right.

✔ *Check Up*

빈칸에 들어갈 알맞은 말을 본문에서 찾아 쓰세요.

Hester Prynne found it difficult to bear the townspeople's ___________________.

정답 : silence

1   처형대는 시민들로 하여금 법에 복종하게 하기 위해 공개적으로 처벌이 행해진 곳이었다.
→ so as to부정사: ~하기 위해서

2   헤스터는 사람들의 야유와 모욕을 마주할 각오가 이미 되어 있었는데도, 그들의 무거운 침묵이 더 참기 힘들다는 것을 알게 됐다. → prepare oneself to부정사: ~할 각오를 하다

3   그녀가 그곳에 서 있을 때, 과거의 기억들이 떠오르기 시작하면서 그녀의 마음은 거슬러 여행을 떠나기 시작했다.

Then Hester Prynne's memories ended, and she found herself back on the scaffolding, surrounded by the townspeople. They were still staring at her and the scarlet letter on her breast. She looked down at the letter on her chest and touched it to assure herself it was real.[1] And it was, as were the infant and her burning shame.

After standing there for a little while, Hester saw a person on the edge of the crowd that she couldn't ignore. He was a white man standing next to a native. The white man, small, with a wrinkled face, was wearing a mix of a civilized and savage costume. Although he had tried to disguise his physical features, it was clear that his left shoulder was higher than his right. As she stared at him, her child cried in pain from the tightness of her grasp on it, but she did not seem to hear.[2]

☐ surrounded by ~에 둘러싸인	☐ savage 야만적인, 사나운
☐ stare at ~을 응시하다	☐ costume (특별한) 복장
☐ assure oneself 납득하다, 확신하다	☐ disguise 변장시키다, 위장시키다
☐ infant 아기, 유아	☐ physical 신체적인
☐ shame 수치, 치욕	☐ feature 특징, 특성
☐ on the edge of ~의 가장자리에	☐ pain 고통
☐ crowd 군중, 무리	☐ tightness 단단함
☐ ignore 무시하다	☐ grasp 움켜잡기, 끌어안기
☐ native 원주민	☐ glance 시선
☐ wrinkled 주름 잡힌	☐ careless 무심한, 무관심한
☐ civilized 교화된, 문명화한	☐ horror 공포

The man, who was a stranger in this town, stared back at Hester Prynne. At first his glance was careless, but as he began to understand the situation she was in, a look of horror came across his face.[3]

본문의 내용과 일치하면 T, 일치하지 않으면 F를 쓰세요.

[a] The man with a native was a citizen of the town. ______

[b] The disguised man was not happy about Hester's situation. ______

정답 : a. F b. T

1 그녀는 가슴 위의 글씨를 내려다보며 그것이 현실이라는 걸 직접 확인하기 위해 글씨를 만졌다.

2 그녀가 그를 응시하고 있을 때, 아기는 그녀가 너무 꼭 끌어안는 바람에 아파서 울었으나, 그녀는 듣지 못하는 듯 했다.

3 처음에 그의 시선은 무심했지만, 그녀가 처한 상황을 파악하기 시작하자 그의 얼굴엔 공포스런 표정이 떠올랐다. → at first: 처음에 / come across: ~에 떠오르다

"I ask you, kind sir," the man said to a townsman, "Who is this woman, and why must she suffer such public shame?"[1]

"You must be a stranger to this town," answered the townsman. "Everyone who lives here knows about Hester Prynne and her wicked ways.[2] She has created a huge scandal among the members of Reverend Dimmesdale's church."

<table>
<tr><td>☐ suffer (고통 등을) 겪다</td><td>☐ hear from ~로부터 소식을 듣다</td></tr>
<tr><td>☐ scandal 추문, 스캔들</td><td>☐ judgment 판단</td></tr>
<tr><td>☐ reverend 목사</td><td>☐ puzzling 헷갈리게 하는, 영문 모를</td></tr>
<tr><td>☐ captive 포로; 포로의</td><td>☐ remain 남아 있다</td></tr>
<tr><td>☐ heathen 이방인, 이교도, 미개인</td><td>☐ refuse to부정사 ~하기를 거절하다</td></tr>
<tr><td>☐ crime 범죄</td><td>☐ name ~의 이름을 대다</td></tr>
<tr><td>☐ scholar 학자</td><td>☐ sinner 죄인</td></tr>
<tr><td>☐ ahead of ~보다 앞서</td><td>☐ mystery 신비, 비밀, 수수께끼</td></tr>
</table>

"That's right," replied the man. "I am a stranger. I have been a captive of the savage heathens in the south for a long time. Please tell me of this woman Hester Prynne's crime."

"This woman is the wife of an English scholar. He decided to join our colony and sent his wife over ahead of him. But this man hasn't been heard from in two years, and his young wife was left to her own poor judgment."[3]

"Ah, I see what you mean," said the stranger with a bitter smile. "So who is the father of the baby she's holding?"

"That fact is the puzzling question that remains for everyone,"[4] said the townsman. "Mrs. Prynne refuses to name the other sinner."

"Her husband should come and solve the mystery," said the stranger.

---

1 이 여인은 누구이며 왜 저런 공개적인 치욕을 겪어야 하는 겁니까?

2 이곳에 사는 사람이라면 누구나 헤스터 프린과 그녀의 부도덕한 행실에 대해 알고 있지요.

3 하지만 이 남자에게서는 2년 동안 소식이 들리지 않았고, 그의 젊은 아내는 자신의 어리석은 판단을 따랐던 거죠. → be left to: ~에 맡겨지다

4 바로 그 사실이 모든 사람들이 궁금해 하는 의문입니다.

"Yes, he should if he's still alive," agreed the townsman. "The penalty for this crime is normally death, but the magistrates were merciful because her husband is probably at the bottom of the sea.[1] But afterward she will bear the scarlet mark of an adulterer for the rest of her life."

"It is a wise punishment," said the stranger. "Her mark will serve as a living sermon against sin. But it angers me that her fellow sinner is not standing there next to her.[2] But he will be discovered and known. He will!"

As the stranger walked away, Hester Prynne kept her eyes on him. She was relieved to be in the presence of the crowd so as not to meet the man alone.[3]

☐ penalty 형벌
☐ merciful 자비로운, 인정 많은
☐ at the bottom of ~의 밑에
☐ bear (흔적 등을) 몸에 지니다, 차다 (bear-bore-borne)
☐ adulterer 간부, 간음한 자
☐ serve as ~로서 알맞다, 쓸모가 있다
☐ sermon 설교
☐ anger 화나게 하다; 화, 노여움
☐ fellow 한 쪽, 맞상대; 녀석, 놈, 동료
☐ discover 발견하다; 밝히다

☐ keep one's eyes on ~에서 눈을 떼지 않다
☐ be relieved 안도하다
☐ in the presence of ~앞에서
☐ be awoken from ~에서 깨어나다
☐ thought 생각, 사고
☐ pronounce 선언하다; 전달하다
☐ governor 주지사
☐ nobleman 귀족
☐ belong to ~에 속하다, ~의 소유다
☐ minister 목사; 장관
☐ pastor (개신교) 사제, 목사

Suddenly, she was awoken from her thoughts by a voice, "Hester Prynne, you must now listen to me!" Standing on the balcony of the nearby church, used by magistrates to pronounce sentences, was Governor Bellingham.[4] There were other noblemen on the balcony with the governor and his men.

Hester Prynne faced the balcony. The voice she had heard belonged to Boston's oldest minister, Pastor John Wilson.

---

1 이런 범죄에 대한 형벌은 보통 사형이지만, 치안 판사들이 자비를 베풀었어요. 그녀의 남편이 바다 밑에 가라앉아 있을지도 모르기 때문이죠.

2 하지만 그녀의 상대였던 죄인이 그녀 옆에 서 있지 않다는 사실이 저를 화나게 만드는군요.

3 그녀는 군중들 앞에 있다는 사실에 안도했다. 그 남자를 혼자 마주 대하지 않아도 되었기 때문이다. → so as not to: ~하지 않기 위해서

4 치안판사들이 판결을 선언할 때 사용하는 근처 교회의 발코니에 벨링햄 주지사가 서 있었다.
   → Standing ... sentences, 가 문두로 와서 주어와 동사가 도치된 문장

"Hester Prynne," continued the old pastor, "I have told your minister here, the Reverend Mr. Dimmsdale, that he should force you to tell us the name of the wicked man who had tempted you to this sad fall here and now."[1]

Then Governor Bellingham spoke, "Good Reverend Dimmesdale, as her minister, you are responsible for this woman's soul. You must urge her to speak and therefore prove her repentance."

To respond, Reverend Dimmesdale rose to address the crowd. The reverend was a young clergyman who had graduated from one of the great English universities. His powerful voice and impressive intellect had already brought him great respect and admiration from the colonists he served.[2]

□ force A to부정사 A에게 ~하라고 강요하다
□ tempt 유혹하다, 꾀다
□ fall 타락
□ here and now 지금 당장에, 즉각
□ be responsible for ~에 책임이 있다
□ soul 영혼
□ urge A to부정사 A가 ~하도록 재촉하다
□ repentance 후회, 회개, 참회
□ clergyman 성직자
□ graduate from ~를 졸업하다
□ impressive 인상적인, 감명을 주는
□ intellect 지력, 지성
□ admiration 감탄, 찬양
□ colonist 식민지 개척자, 식민지 주민
□ misplaced 잘못된, 엉뚱한
□ pity 동정, 연민
□ tenderness 마음이 무름; 유연함
□ affect 영향을 미치다, 감동시키다
□ expression 표정; 표현
□ entreaty 간청, 탄원, 애원
□ shake one's head 머리를 가로젓다
  (shake-shook-shaken)

"Speak to the woman, brother," urged Pastor Wilson. "You are the only one who can save her soul!"

Reverend Dimmesdale looked to the woman on the scaffolding. "Hester Prynne," he began. "You've heard what the good Pastor Wilson has said. I urge you to speak the name of your fellow sinner. It will give both of your hearts peace. Do not remain silent out of misplaced pity or tenderness for him!"[3]

Even the baby in Hester Prynne's arms was affected by the reverend's powerful voice. It looked up at him with a half-happy, half-sad expression on its face. But to this entreaty, Hester just shook her head.

✔ Check Up

What does Hester Prynne have to do in order to save her soul?

[a] She must give up her baby to the true father.
[b] She must marry the father of her baby.
[c] She must tell the townspeople who the father of her baby is.

정답 : c

---

1 나는 여기 있는 당신의 담임 목사 딤스데일에게 당신을 이런 슬픈 타락의 길로 유혹한 부도덕한 남자의 이름을 지금 당장 우리에게 말하게 해야 한다고 했소.

2 힘 있는 목소리와 인상 깊은 지성 덕분에 그는 이미 자신이 봉사하는 식민지 주민들에게서 엄청난 존경과 찬양을 받고 있었다.

3 그에 대한 잘못된 동정심이나 약한 마음 때문에 침묵을 지켜서는 안 됩니다.
→ remain + 형용사: ~한 채로 있다

"Woman, do not test the limits of Heaven's mercy!" said Pastor Wilson with an angry voice. "Speak the name, and your repentance will be enough to take the scarlet letter off your breast!"[1]

- ☐ limit 한계
- ☐ mercy 자비
- ☐ remove 제거하다
- ☐ endure 견디다, 참다
- ☐ agony 심한 고통, 고뇌
- ☐ seem to부정사 ~하는 것처럼 보이다
- ☐ recognize 알아보다, 인식하다
- ☐ stern 가혹한; (표정 등이) 엄한
- ☐ insist 고집하다, 우기다
- ☐ earthly 이 세상의, 속세의
- ☐ heavenly 하늘의; 천국의
- ☐ confess 고백하다
- ☐ whisper 속삭이다
- ☐ lean 기대다; 몸을 구부리다

1 이름을 말하시오. 그러면 당신의 회개로 가슴에서 주홍글씨를 족히 뗄 수 있을 거요!
→ be enough to부정사: ~하기에 충분하다

"Never!" shouted Hester Prynne. She looked deeply into Reverend Dimmesdale's eyes. "This letter is branded too deeply on my heart to remove it so easily. I hope to endure his agony as well as my own!"

"Speak!" cried the townspeople around the scaffolding. "Speak the name of your baby's father!"

She went pale as she seemed to recognize one of the stern, cold voices coming from the crowd.[2] But she insisted, "I will not speak. My baby will never have an earthly father. She will have to know the heavenly one!"

"She won't confess his name," whispered Dimmsdale, as he leaned over the balcony with his hand over his heart.[3] "She will not speak!" he announced to the crowd.

---

2 군중 속에서 흘러나오는 가혹하고 차가운 목소리들 중 하나를 알아차린 듯 했을 때 그녀는 창백해졌다.

3 "그녀는 그의 이름을 고백하지 않을 겁니다." 하고 딤스데일은 자신의 가슴에 한 손을 얹은 채 발코니 너머로 몸을 기울이며 속삭였다.

One Point

I hope to endure his agony **as well as** my own!
제 고통뿐만 아니라 그의 고통도 견뎌내고 싶습니다!

A as well as B: B뿐만 아니라 A도 (= not only B but also A)
ex. I hate you **as well as** your father. 난 당신 아버지뿐만 아니라 당신도 증오해요.

Once Hester had returned to the prison, she was in a state of nervous hysteria. And the baby kept crying wildly. Master Brackett, the jailer, kept a constant watch on her to make sure she did not hurt herself or her baby.[1] Finally, he brought in a doctor to see her. The doctor was the same stranger who had taken an interest in her while she had been on the scaffolding.[2] His name was Roger Chillingworth.

As the jailer led him into the room and Hester Prynne saw him, she became as still as death.[3]

"Don't worry," the doctor told the jailer. "I'll take great care of Mrs. Prynne and her child. You will soon have peace and quiet in your prison."

The doctor mixed up an herbal remedy from local plants that he had learned from the natives.[4]

"Here Mrs. Prynne, give this to your baby. She'll only accept it from your hands, and it will calm her."

☐ state 상태, 형편	☐ remedy 치료, 치료약
☐ nervous 초조한, 긴장한	☐ calm 달래다, 가라앉히다
☐ hysteria 히스테리, 병적 흥분	☐ avenge oneself 복수하다
☐ jailer 교도관, 간수	☐ poison 독살하다; 독약
☐ keep a watch on ~을 지키다	☐ innocent 천진난만한, 죄 없는
☐ constant 끊임없는	☐ soothing 달래는, 진정시키는
☐ make sure 확인하다	☐ manner 태도
☐ take an interest in ~에 관심을 가지다	☐ harm 해치다
☐ take care of ~을 돌보다	☐ misbegotten 사생아의
☐ mix up 잘 섞다	☐ hesitantly 주저하며
☐ herbal 풀의, 약초의	☐ drop off to sleep (어느새) 잠들다

Hester pushed his hand away. "Would you avenge yourself by poisoning this innocent baby?" she whispered.

"Woman, don't be foolish!" the doctor responded in a cold yet soothing manner. "I would not harm this poor, misbegotten baby."

Hesitantly, she gave the drink to her infant, and it dropped peacefully off to sleep.

✔ *Check Up*

빈칸에 들어갈 알맞은 말을 본문에서 찾아 쓰세요.

The doctor gave an _______________ drink to Hester to make her baby sleep.

정답 : herbal

1 간수장 브라켓은 그녀가 자신이나 아기를 해치지 못하도록 계속 그녀를 감시했다.

2 그 의사는 그녀가 처형대 위에 있는 동안 그녀에게 관심을 보였던 바로 그 이방인이었다.

3 간수장이 그를 감방 안으로 데리고 와 헤스터 프린이 그를 보자, 그녀는 죽은 듯이 꼼짝하지 않았다. → as still as death: 쥐죽은 듯 조용한, 매우 잠잠한

4 그 의사는 원주민들에게서 배운, 지방 고유의 식물에서 추출한 약초 치료제를 만들었다.

Then the doctor offered Hester some medicine for herself. Looking warily into the cup, she said, "And how do I know you wouldn't kill me with poison for revenge?"

"Hester," responded the doctor, "do you know me so little that you think my purposes could be so shallow? Would not letting you live with this burning shame on your breast be the best revenge of all?"[1]

At this, she smiled a little and took her medicine. The doctor continued speaking while her medicine took effect. "You know, I should have guessed this would have happened. I could have seen that scarlet letter blazing at the end of the church aisle we walked down on the day we got married."

☐ offer 제공하다; 제안하다	☐ wrong 나쁜 짓을 하다
☐ medicine 약	☐ trap 덫으로 잡다, 함정에 빠뜨리다
☐ warily 조심하여, 방심 않고	☐ blossoming 꽃 피는
☐ revenge 복수	☐ youth 젊음
☐ shallow 얕은, 얄팍한	☐ unnatural 부자연스러운
☐ take effect 효력을 나타내다	☐ bond 유대, 맺음; 약정, 계약
☐ guess 추측하다	☐ decay 부식, 쇠퇴
☐ blaze 타오르다; 불꽃, 섬광	☐ scale 저울
☐ aisle 통로, 복도	☐ cowardly 비겁한, 겁 많은
☐ pretend to부정사 ~하는 체하다	☐ identity 정체, 신원

"You know," she said to him, "I was always honest with you. I always told you I felt no love for you, nor would I ever pretend to. But I am sorry. I have greatly wronged you."

"No," he answered, "We have wronged each other. I should not have trapped your blossoming youth into this unnatural bond with my decay. The scales between us are balanced. But I will seek revenge against the cowardly man who has left you to suffer this shame alone.[2] You might not tell me his name, but I will discover it. I will! Now all I ask you is that you keep my identity as your husband a secret in this town.[3] And do not tell the man upon whom I'll seek revenge about me."

"I will keep your secret as I have his," said Hester.

1 당신이 가슴에 이 강렬한 치욕을 달고 살게 하는 게 무엇보다도 최고의 복수가 아니겠소?

2 하지만 나는 당신 혼자 이런 치욕을 겪도록 내버려둔 그 겁쟁이에게 복수할 거요.

3 이제 내가 당신에게 부탁하는 건 당신의 남편이라는 내 정체를 이 마을에서 비밀로 해달라는 것뿐이오. → keep A a secret: A를 비밀로 하다

One Point

You know, I **should have guessed** this would have happened.
이런 일이 일어날 거라는 걸 알았어야 했는데.

should have + 과거분사: ~했어야 했는데 → 과거의 일에 대한 후회나 원망이 담겨 있다.

ex. You **should have gone** to the party. 넌 그 파티에 갔어야 했어.

Comprehension Quiz

A 등장인물과 그에 대한 설명으로 맞는 것을 짝지으세요.

❶ Hester Prynne · · ⓐ the man Hester Prynne married

❷ Pastor Wilson · · ⓑ a magistrate in Boston colony

❸ Roger Chillingworth · · ⓒ the oldest minister in Boston colony

❹ Governor Bellingham · · ⓓ a handsome young minister with a powerful voice

❺ Reverend Dimmesdale · · ⓔ a tall woman with an elegant figure

B 다음 중 밑줄 친 표현이 올바르게 쓰인 것을 고르세요.

❶ (a) She <u>gathered</u> a scarlet letter on her breast.

(b) The townspeople <u>gathered</u> outside the prison.

❷ (a) The baby <u>ushered</u> when it saw the sunlight.

(b) With his hand, he tried to <u>usher</u> out a young woman.

❸ (a) That fact is the <u>puzzling</u> question that remains for everyone.

(b) The old man was <u>puzzling</u> a look in her eye.

Answers

A ❶ – ⓔ ❷ – ⓒ ❸ – ⓐ ❹ – ⓑ ❺ – ⓓ

B ❶ (b) ❷ (b) ❸ (a)

C 다음 질문에 맞는 답을 고르세요.

1 What did the scarlet A on Hester Prynne's bosom stand for?

(a) Alphabet　　　(b) Adulterer　　　(c) Admirable

2 What fact did Roger Chillingworth make Hester Prynne swear to conceal?

(a) That he was not a real doctor

(b) That he was the father of her baby

(c) That he was her husband

D 보기에서 알맞은 단어를 골라 다음 문장을 완성하세요.

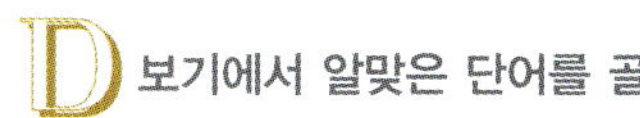

> fanciful　merciful　sermon　spikes　misbegotten

1 Her mark will serve as a living _____________ against sin.

2 Then the prison door, covered in iron _____________, flew open.

3 The design was artistic and _____________.

4 The penalty for this crime is normally death, but the magistrates were _____________.

5 I would not harm this poor, _____________ baby.

---

*A*nswers

C　**1** (b)　**2** (c)

D　**1** sermon　**2** spikes　**3** fanciful　**4** merciful　**5** misbegotten

CHAPTER TWO

Hester's Pearl

The imprisonment of Hester Prynne ended shortly after her discussion with the doctor, but the torment of her life among the townspeople was just beginning.[1]

She was free to leave the town. But Hester had decided to stay and face her lifelong sentence. She and her baby moved into a small cottage on the outskirts of town. She was able to make a decent living with her expert sewing skills. But she spent very little of her income on herself. She dressed her young daughter very well and gave her extra money to charity.

☐ pearl 진주
☐ imprisonment 투옥, 구금, 금고
☐ discussion 토론, 토의
☐ torment 고통, 고뇌; 고문
☐ be free to 부정사 자유롭게 ~할 수 있다
☐ cottage 오두막
☐ on the outskirts of ~의 변두리에
☐ make a living 생계를 세우다
☐ decent 남부럽지 않은; (수입이) 상당한
☐ expert 숙련된, 노련한

☐ income 수입
☐ charity 자선(행위); 자애, 자비
☐ exceptional 예외적인; 특별한, 비범한
☐ hire 고용하다
☐ allow A to 부정사 A가 ~하는 걸 허락하다
☐ nevertheless 그럼에도 불구하고
☐ perceive 지각하다; 이해하다
☐ behavior 행동
☐ connect 연결하다
☐ influence 영향을 끼치다

Because of her exceptional skill, the townspeople always hired Hester to do work. But they never allowed her to forget her shame with their looks and words.

Hester's daughter, Pearl, had been named not for a pearl's great beauty or value, but rather for its great price.[2] Nevertheless, the baby soon blossomed into a beautiful but strange child. When Hester watched her daughter and perceived the young girl's strange behavior, she worried that the child was somehow also connected and influenced by the scarlet letter.

How did Hester Prynne make a living?

a She took care of some young girls from the town.

b She worked as a seamstress.

c She sold pearls that she found on the beach.

정답 : q

---

1   헤스터 프린의 수감생활은 그 의사와의 상담 직후 끝났지만, 마을 사람들 틈에서의 고통스러운 삶은 이제 막 시작되었다.

2   헤스터의 딸 펄은 진주의 뛰어난 아름다움이나 가치 때문이 아니라 그 위대한 희생 때문에 붙여진 이름이다. → not A but B: A가 아니라 B

As Pearl got older, it became clear that the child could not be forced to adapt to rules. She would not heed the simplest of her mother's commands. And her temper were uneven. It was as if the warfare of Hester's spirit were carrying on in Pearl.

Hester would have liked to see her playing with other children. But Pearl was as much an outcast as her mother, and she accepted her position from the time when she was very young. Fate had built an unbreakable wall around Pearl. When she did meet some of the town's vicious Puritan children, who gathered around her, she would become terrible, flinging stones at them and screaming like a small savage.[1]

The sight of her combative daughter brought Hester to her knees, asking, "Dear Heavenly Father, what kind of being is this that I've brought into the

□ adapt to ~에 적응하다
□ heed 주의[조심]하다
□ command 명령, 지시
□ temper 성질, 기질
□ uneven 고르지 않은
□ warfare 전쟁, 교전 상태
□ spirit 정신
□ outcast 추방자; 쫓겨난, 버림 받은
□ position 위치, 지위
□ fate 운명
□ unbreakable 깨지지 않는
□ vicious 악의 있는, 심술궂은, 사악한
□ fling 던지다 (fling-flung-flung)
□ scream 비명을 지르다
□ combative 투쟁적인, 싸우기 좋아하는
□ merely 그저, 단순히
□ elf-like 요정 같은
□ intelligence 지능, 지성
□ attraction 매력, 사람의 마음을 끄는 것
□ bosom 가슴

world?" And when little Pearl heard her mother cry like this, she would merely look at her and smile with her elf-like intelligence.

One of the strangest things about Pearl was that as a baby, her first interest had not been her mother's smile, as it is with most infants.[2] Rather her first attraction was to the scarlet A on her mother's bosom.

---

1 그녀는 자기 주변에 모여든 마을의 심술궂은 청교도 아이들과 맞닥뜨리면, 작은 야만인처럼 그들에게 돌을 던지고 소리를 지르며 못되게 변했다.

2 펄에게서 가장 이상한 것 중 하나는, 아기였을 때 그녀가 처음 관심을 보인 것이 대부분의 아기들과는 달리 엄마의 미소가 아니었다는 것이다.

One Point

It was **as if** the warfare of Hester's spirit were carrying on in Pearl.
마치 헤스터의 영혼의 전쟁이 펄의 내면에서 벌어지고 있는 것 같았다.

- -

as if + 가정법: 마치 ~처럼

ex. It seemed **as if** I were dreaming. 마치 내가 꿈을 꾸는 것 같았어요.

Some years later, Pearl was running around. One day, she gathered a bundle of wildflowers. She then began pitching them at the letter on her mother's breast and dancing up and down with joy when one of them hit the scarlet letter.[1]

□ a bundle of 한 다발의	□ flash 번쩍이다; 번쩍임
□ pitch 던지다	□ demonic 악마의, 악마 같은
□ instinct 본능	□ playfully 농담으로
□ resist 저항하다, 참다	□ serious 진지한, 심각한
□ consider 생각하다, 고려하다	□ after a pause 잠시 후에
□ painful 고통스러운	□ hesitation 주저, 망설임
□ strike 부딪침; 부딪치다	□ keen 날카로운
□ penance 참회, 후회, 고행	□ shudder 떨다; 몸서리치다
□ obvious 명백한, 대번에 알 수 있는	□ unable to ~할 수 없는

Hester's first instinct was to cover the letter with her arms. But she resisted, considering each flower's painful strike against her heart to be part of her penance.[2] To her mother's obvious pain, Pearl only laughed, her eyes flashing with a demonic glow.

"Are you really my child?" Hester asked her playfully. "Who made you, and who sent you here?"

"You tell me," replied Pearl, who became very serious. "Do tell me."

"The Heavenly Father sent you," Hester answered after a pause.

But her hesitation was not lost on the child's keen intelligence.[3] "He did not send me," cried Pearl. "I have no Heavenly Father!"

"Oh please," cried Hester. "You mustn't say that. He created all of us!"

"No, you must tell me," laughed Pearl, who danced about. "Do tell me!"

Hester shuddered, unable to answer her question.

---

1 그리고는 엄마의 가슴 위에 있는 글씨를 향해 그것을 던지며 그 중 하나가 주홍글씨에 맞으면 기뻐서 깡충깡충 춤을 추었다. → with joy: 기뻐서

2 그러나 그녀는 자기 가슴에 꽃이 고통스럽게 부딪히는 것을 속죄의 일부라 여기며 참아냈다.

3 하지만 영리한 아이는 엄마가 망설이는 것을 놓치지 않았다.

One day, Hester brought Pearl with her to Governor Bellingham's mansion. She told Pearl they were going to return a pair of gloves he had asked her to embroider, but the real reason was that Hester had heard rumors that the townspeople were planning to take her daughter away from her.[1]

They suspected Pearl might be a demon child, so by taking her away, they planned to save Hester's soul. Hester had also heard that Governor Bellingham was at the head of this plan. So she made up her mind to speak with him.

That day, she had dressed Pearl in a bright red dress that was embroidered with gold thread, just like her scarlet A, so that the child seemed to be a living extension of it.[2]

□ mansion 대저택
□ reason 이유
□ rumor 소문
□ suspect 의심하다
□ demon 악마, 귀신
□ at the head of ~의 선두에 서서
□ make up one's mind to부정사
　~하기로 결심하다

□ extension 연장, 확장
□ luxurious 사치스러운, 호화로운
□ rosebush 장미덤불
□ demand 요구하다, 요청하다
□ pick (꽃 등을) 꺾다
□ burst into 갑자기 ~하기 시작하다
　(burst-burst-burst)
□ fit 발작, 경련

38

When they reached the luxurious mansion, Pearl saw a blossoming rosebush and demanded that her mother pick one of the red flowers for her.[3]

Check Up 본문의 내용과 일치하면 T, 일치하지 않으면 F를 쓰세요.

a Hester suspected that the Governor planned to take Pearl away from her. _____
b Hester went to the Governor's mansion to return a pair of gloves. _____

정답 : a. T b. F

1 그녀는 그가 수를 놓아 달라고 부탁한 장갑을 돌려 주러 가는 거라고 펄에게 말했지만, 진짜 이유는 마을 사람들이 딸을 그녀에게서 **빼앗아** 갈 계획이라는 소문을 들었기 때문이다.
→ take A away from B: B에게서 A를 빼앗다

2 그날 그녀는 펄에게 그녀의 주홍색 A자처럼 금실로 수놓아진 밝은 빨간 색 드레스를 입혔다. 그래서 아이는 그것(주홍글씨)이 생명을 지녀 커진 것처럼 보였다.

3 호화로운 저택에 도착했을 때, 펄은 활짝 핀 장미덤불을 보고는 엄마에게 빨간 꽃 한 송이를 꺾어 달라고 요구했다.

When Hester refused, Pearl burst into a fit of tears and let out an ear-piercing scream. But she then suddenly became silent when she saw some people approaching them.

In the group were Governor Bellingham, Pastor Wilson, the young Reverend Arthur Dimmesdale, and Doctor Roger Chillingworth. Reverend Dimmesdale's health had been suffering as of late, and the doctor, who was treating him, had become his close and constant companion.[1]

Looking with surprise at the little girl dressed in stunning scarlet, the governor asked, "Who is this little one here?"

"Ah, this is the daughter of the unfortunate Hester Prynne," Pastor Wilson said. "She is the one we've spoken about recently."

□ ear-piercing 귓전을 때리는
□ approach 다가오다, 접근하다
□ treat 치료하다; 다루다
□ constant <문어> 충실한; 지속적인
□ companion 동료, 친구, 벗
□ stunning 멋진, 매력적인
□ look into ~을 조사하다
□ matter 문제
□ directly 똑바로, 직접

□ as to ~에 대해서
□ duty 의무, 임무
□ protect 보호하다, 지키다
□ eternal 영원한
□ clothe 의복을 지급하다; 입히다
□ plainly 검소하게
□ discipline 훈련하다
□ badge 상징; 배지
□ righteous (도덕적으로) 바른

"Yes," said Governor Bellingham. "We shall look into this matter right here and now. Hester Prynne," he said, looking directly at the letter on her breast, "we have greatly discussed as to whether it is our duty to protect the eternal souls of you and your child.[2] Don't you think it would be best for this child to be taken and clothed plainly and disciplined in the truths of Heaven and Earth?"[3]

"I can teach my daughter better than anyone else," said Hester Prynne, putting her finger on her letter. "I have learned from this."

"Woman," said the governor, "that is your badge of shame, and the reason we think it best to put the child in more righteous hands."[4]

---

1 최근에 딤스데일 목사의 건강이 악화되고 있어서, 그를 치료하던 의사는 그의 가깝고도 충실한 동반자가 되었다. → as of late: 최근에

2 우리는 당신과 당신 아이의 영혼을 보호하는 것이 우리의 의무가 아닌지에 대해 많은 논의를 했소.

3 이 아이를 데려가 수수하게 옷을 입히고 하늘과 땅의 진리 속에서 교육을 받게 하는 것이 최선이라고 생각하지 않소?

4 그것은 당신의 치욕에 대한 상징이며, 우리가 그 아이를 보다 올바른 손에 맡기는 것이 최선이라고 생각하는 이유요.

"Nevertheless," Hester Prynne said calmly, "it has taught me lessons which will make my daughter wiser and better."

"We will be the judges of that," said Bellingham. Then he sat down in a chair and tried to put Pearl between his knees, but the child, unaccustomed to the touch of anyone but her mother, escaped.[1]

Pastor Wilson, who was known to be good with children, continued the examination, "Pearl, can you tell me who made you?"

<table>
<tr><td>☐ unaccustomed to ~에 익숙하지 않은</td><td>☐ mischievously 장난기 있게</td></tr>
<tr><td>☐ escape 도망치다</td><td>☐ pluck 잡아뜯다, 뽑다</td></tr>
<tr><td>☐ examination 조사, 검사; 시험</td><td>☐ grab 움켜 잡다 (grab-grabbed-grabbed)</td></tr>
<tr><td>☐ educate 교육시키다</td><td>☐ in return 보답으로</td></tr>
<tr><td>☐ belief 신념, 믿음</td><td>☐ torture 고문; 심한 고통</td></tr>
<tr><td>☐ creation 창조</td><td>☐ care for ~을 돌보다</td></tr>
</table>

Hester Prynne had educated her child at home in the matters of Puritan beliefs about the creation of the human spirit.[2] But Pearl decided to answer the serious question mischievously. She then announced that she had not been made in Heaven, but rather she had been plucked from the wild rosebush that grew by the prison door.[3]

"This is terrible," the governor cried. "Here is a three-year-old child who can't tell who made her!"

Hester Prynne grabbed Pearl into her arms, "God gave me this child in return for all the things he has taken from me. She is my happiness and my torture! I will die before you take her from me!"

"Child," said old Pastor Wilson, "Pearl will be cared for better than you can do!"

✔ Check Up

Where do the Puritans believe people are made?

a In a woman's womb

b In nature

c In Heaven

정답 : c

---

1 그런 다음 그는 의자에 앉아서 펄을 자신의 무릎 사이에 두려고 했지만, 엄마 이외에 어느 누구의 손길에도 익숙하지 않았던 아이는 달아났다. → but: ~을 제외하고

2 헤스터 프린은 집에서 인간 영혼의 창조에 대한 청교도적인 믿음을 아이에게 교육시켰다.

3 그래서 그녀는 자기가 하늘에서 만들어진 게 아니라 감옥 문 옆에서 자라는 야생 장미 덤불에서 뽑혔다고 말했다.

"God gave her to me for safekeeping!" screamed Hester Prynne. Then she turned to the young Reverend Dimmesdale and cried, "You speak for me! You were my pastor and in charge of my soul![1] You know me better than these men can! Don't let them take her away from me!"

"There is truth in her words," Reverend Dimmesdale said in his powerful, trembling voice. "God gave this child to this mother to teach her to change her wicked ways. That bond is sacred. Who are we to say that God made a mistake in giving the child to her?[2] Who are we to take away the good Lord's one blessing in her life?"

"Well spoken," said Pastor Wilson. "What do you say, Governor Bellingham? The good reverend has pleaded convincingly on Hester Prynne's behalf."

"Indeed he has," answered the governor. "Pearl shall stay with her mother, and we will make no fur-

□ safekeeping 보관, 보호	□ plead 변호하다, 항변하다
□ trembling 떨리는	□ convincingly 설득력 있게
□ sacred 신성한	□ on one's behalf ~을 대신하여, ~을 위하여
□ make a mistake 실수하다	□ indeed 실지로
□ the Lord 하나님	□ proper 적당한
□ blessing 축복, 은혜	□ cheek 뺨

1 저 대신 말씀 좀 해주세요! 당신은 제 담임 목사였으니 제 영혼에 대해 책임이 있으셨어요!
 → in charge of: ~을 맡고 있는

ther scandal of the matter.[3] At the proper time, the church's officers will make sure that she goes to school and church. That's all."

Then young Pearl grabbed Reverend Dimmesdale's hand and put it on her cheek. The minister looked around and then kissed her forehead.

✔ *Check Up*

What did Reverend Dimmesdale NOT say about why Hester should keep Pearl?

　a Pearl is the one blessing in Hester's life.
　b There is a sacred bond between a mother and her daughter.
　c Hester can teach Pearl better than anyone else can.

정답: c

2 우리가 뭔데 신이 그녀에게 아이를 선물하는 실수를 저질렀다고 말합니까?

3 펄은 자기 어머니와 함께 있을 것이고, 우린 이 문제에 대해 더 이상 소란을 피우지 않을 것이오.

"A strange child," said Doctor Chillingworth. "Perhaps if we study her nature, we'll be able to guess the identity of her sinful father."[1]

"It would be sinful to do that," answered Pastor Wilson. "It would be better to pray on the matter and leave it to God's will."

☐ nature 본성, 천성	☐ witchcraft 마법, 요술
☐ sinful 죄가 있는, 죄 많은	☐ hiss 쉿 하는 소리를 내다
☐ pray （신에게) 빌다, 간청하다	☐ congregation 모임, 집회
☐ settle 해결하다	☐ the Black Man 악마
☐ execute 처형하다; 실행하다	☐ evil 사악한, 부도덕한
☐ practice 실행하다, 연습하다	☐ Satan 악마

1 만약 우리가 그 아이의 천성을 자세히 살핀다면, 그 아이의 죄 많은 아버지의 정체를 추측해낼 수 있을 겁니다. → will be able to부정사: ~할 수 있을 것이다

After the matter was settled, Hester Prynne and Pearl left the governor's mansion. Outside the house they met Mistress Hibbins, Governor Bellingham's bitter sister, who was executed a few years later for practicing witchcraft.[2]

"Hst hst," she hissed. "Will you two come with us to the forest tonight to hold congregation with the Black Man?"

"We will not!" answered Hester Prynne. "I will stay at home with my daughter. But if they had taken her from me, I would have come with you and signed my name in the evil Black Man's book in my own blood!"

After this, it could be said that even this early, the child had saved Hester Prynne's soul from Satan's trap.[3]

✔ *Check Up*

How did Pearl save her mother's soul?

a Pearl taught Hester about God's forgiveness.

b Pearl was the reason Hester did not join Mistress Hibbins.

c Pearl convinced her mother to sign her name in the Black Man's book.

정답 : q

2 집 밖에서 그들은 벨링햄 주지사의 못된 여동생 히빈스 부인을 만났는데, 그녀는 불과 몇 년 후 마법을 부렸다는 이유로 처형되었다.

3 이것을 보면, 아이가 그렇게 빠른 시기에 악마의 덫에서 헤스터 프린의 영혼을 구했다고 말할 수 있을 것이다.

《주홍글씨》의 근간을 이루는 것은 메이플라워호를 타고 북아메리카에 간 뉴잉글랜드 이민과 청교도입니다. 이에 대해 좀 더 알아봅시다.

About Puritans and Pilgrim

청교도들과 필그림

Most American high school students learn that the first Pilgrims came from England, and this is true to a certain degree. Most of these Pilgrims actually came from Holland, where they lived for a while after leaving England. The Pilgrims were Puritans who believed that everyone should be highly educated, and that any one of their members could be elected to high positions in the church. The English monarchy did not like these ideas, as they were actually similar to a democratic form of government.

the Pilgrims 영국 망명교도들   degree 수준, 정도   Puritan 청교도   educate 교육하다   elect 선출하다   monarchy 군주제   democratic 민주적인   strict 엄격한   pure 순수한, 고결한   corrupt 타락시키다, 부패시키다   remote 외진, 멀리 떨어진   fit 적당한   served as ~의 역할을 하다

대부분의 미국 고등학생들은 최초의 필그림들이 영국에서 왔다고 배웁니다. 어느 정도는 맞는 얘기죠. 사실, 이들 필그림들은 대부분 네덜란드에서 왔답니다. 그들이 영국을 떠나 한동안 살던 곳이지요. 필그림들은 청교도입니다. 그들은 모든 사람이 고등 교육을 받아야 하고, 그들의 일원 중 어느 누구든 교회에서 고위직에 선출될 수 있다고 믿었습니다. 영국의 군주제는 이런 생각을 마음에 들어 하지 않았습니다. 그것은 사실상 민주적인 정부 형태와 유사했기 때문입니다.

However, the Puritans were not political. They were more interested in living according to their strict and pure religion. The Puritans left England for Holland, but they did not like living there, either. They were afraid that the Dutch influence would corrupt weaker members of their Puritan community. They wanted to live in a remote area, where they would be free not only to live their lives as they saw fit, but also to control others and to force them to live a

strict Puritan lifestyle also. They were successful in creating this type of society after coming to the New World, and this is the setting for the "Scarlet Letter."

Actually, their ideas served as some of the basic, founding ideas of the American nation many, many years after the Pilgrims arrived in the New World.

하지만 청교도인들은 정치적이지는 않았습니다. 그들은 엄격하고 고결한 종교에 따라 사는 것에 보다 관심이 있었습니다. 청교도인들은 영국을 떠나 네덜란드로 갔지만, 거기서 사는 것도 좋아하지 않았습니다. 그들은 네덜란드의 영향력이 청교도 사회의 심지가 약한 일원들을 타락시킬까봐 두려웠기 때문이죠. 그들은 외진 곳에서 살고 싶었습니다. 그들이 옳다고 생각하는 대로 자유로이 살 수 있을 뿐만 아니라, 다른 이들을 통제해 그들 또한 엄격한 청교도 생활방식으로 살게 만들 수 있는 그런 곳 말이죠. 그들은 신세계로 온 이후 이런 유형의 사회를 만드는 데 성공했습니다. 그리고 그곳이 바로 《주홍글씨》의 무대죠.

실제로 그들의 사상은 필그림들이 신세계에 온 지 많은 세월이 흐른 후 미국의 기본적인 건국 이념 중 일부가 되었습니다.

Revenge

It was around the time that Roger Chillingworth settled in the town as a doctor that the young Reverend Dimmesdale's health began to decline. The townspeople saw the coincidence of the ailing reverend and the doctor's arrival as a miracle enacted by the providence of God.[1] Therefore the town elders thought it was God's will that reverend Dimmesdale's health be placed in Dr. Chillingworth's hands.

The two men soon became constant companions. Reverend Dimmesdale was fascinated by Chillingworth's

☐ decline 쇠퇴하다, (힘이) 쇠하다	☐ clue 실마리, 단서
☐ coincidence 우연의 일치	☐ be convinced 확신하다
☐ ailing 병든, 앓고 있는	☐ result 결과
☐ arrival 도착; 등장, 출현	☐ troubled 근심스러운, 불안한
☐ miracle 기적	☐ figure out 이해하다, 해결하다
☐ enact 제정하다, 규정하다	☐ demeanor 태도, 몸가짐
☐ providence 섭리, 신의 뜻	☐ remarkably 현저하게, 몹시, 매우
☐ a wealth of 수많은, 풍부한	☐ cause 야기시키다, ~의 원인이 되다
☐ look for ~을 찾다	☐ haunt ~을 따라다니다; ~에 출몰하다

wealth of experience as a doctor and an older man, while the doctor spent his time looking for clues to the reverend's illness.[2] Chillingworth was convinced that his bodily sickness was the result of a troubled heart and mind. Yet the doctor was unable to figure out just what was troubling the reverend's mind.

The two men soon moved into a house together. But as time passed, the townspeople began to see Doctor Chillingworth differently. His appearance and demeanor had changed remarkably since moving to the town. Where he was once calm and kind, they now saw evil on his face.[3] Rumors around town said that the reverend's poor health was caused by Satan, who haunted him in the form of Roger Chillingworth.

---

1 마을 사람들은 아픈 목사와 의사의 등장이라는 우연의 일치를 신의 섭리로 이루어진 기적이라고 생각했다.

2 딤스데일 목사가 칠링워스의 의사로서 그리고 연장자로서의 풍부한 경험에 매료된 사이, 의사는 목사의 병에 대한 실마리를 찾으며 시간을 보냈다. → be fascinated by: ~에 매료되다

3 한때 그는 차분하고 친절했지만, 이제 그들은 그의 얼굴에서 악의를 보았다.
→ where: <문어> ~하는데, ~하는 데 반해

It happened one day that the reverend visited Chillingworth in his laboratory, where he often made drugs from plants he had collected. The doctor was examining a bundle of ugly-looking plants from the graveyard that stood next to their house.[1]

"I found these leaves in that graveyard right there," said the doctor, pointing out the window. "This variety is new to me. I found them growing out of an unmarked grave. I suspect they grew out of the man's heart. Perhaps they represent a dreadful secret that he was buried with. It would have been better that he confessed it during his lifetime."[2]

"Maybe he wanted to but was unable," said the reverend, gripping his breast as if it were throbbing with pain. "When the members of my church confess their sins, they are always greatly relieved."

□ laboratory 실험실	□ throb 욱신욱신 쑤시다; 고동치다
□ collect 모으다, 수집하다	□ footpath 보도, 좁은 길
□ graveyard 묘지	□ disrespectfully 무례하게, 실례되게
□ variety 변종; 다양	□ skip 뛰어다니다, 깡충깡충 뛰다
□ unmarked 표지가 없는	□ tomb 무덤, 묘
□ grave 무덤, 묘	□ a handful of 한 움큼의, 한 줌의
□ represent 나타내다	□ prickly 가시투성이의, 바늘이 있는
□ dreadful 무서운, 두려운	□ burr 가시 돋친 껍질[식물] (= bur)
□ bury 묻다, 매장하다	□ burdock 우엉
□ grip 꽉 잡다, 움켜잡다	□ stick 찌르다, 찔러 넣다 (stick-stuck-stuck)

Just then the doctor and the reverend saw Hester Prynne and Pearl walking over a footpath that ran through the graveyard. Pearl was disrespectfully skipping along from the top of one tomb to the next. Then she gathered a handful of prickly burrs from a burdock plant and stuck them along the lines of her mother's scarlet A.[3]

✔ Check Up

빈칸에 들어갈 알맞은 말을 본문에서 찾아 쓰세요.

He would not _______________ his mistake, even though everyone knew he was guilty of it.

정답 : confess

1 의사는 자기 집 옆에 있는 묘지에서 채집한 한 다발의 흉측하게 생긴 식물들을 살펴보고 있었다.

2 살아 있는 동안 그것을 고백하는 게 나았을 텐데.
　→ would have + 과거분사: <가정법> ~했을 텐데

3 그런 다음 그 아이는 우엉 식물에서 가시투성이의 우엉을 한 줌 모아 엄마의 주홍색 A자 라인을 따라 찔러 넣었다.

"Ah, that child has no respect for law or authority," said Roger Chillingworth. "Just the other day I saw her splash water from a horse trough on the governor. What in Heaven's name is wrong with her?"

Suddenly, Pearl ran up to the window and threw one of the prickly burrs at Reverend Dimmesdale. Then she laughed and called to her mother, "Let's go, Mother. Or the Black Man is going to get you like he

□ respect 존경심
□ law 법
□ authority 권위
□ splash (물 등을) 튀기다
□ trough 구유, 여물통
□ miserable 비참한, 불쌍한
□ judgment 판단
□ cause 원인
□ chronic 만성적인
□ ailment 병; 불쾌
□ frankly speaking 솔직히 말해서
□ fail to부정사 ~하지 못하다, 실패하다

has already gotten the reverend.[1] Come quickly, or he'll catch you! But he can't catch me!"

"Do you think Hester Prynne is less miserable for bearing her shame in that letter on her breast, rather than hiding it away in her heart?"[2] the doctor asked the reverend as the mother and her child walked away from the window.

"Yes, I believe so," answered the reverend. "But what I really want to talk about right now is my health. What is your judgment as to the cause of my chronic ailment?"

"Frankly speaking," said the doctor, "I want to know if you have any secrets you're failing to tell me.[3] Have you told me everything about your problems?"

What did Pearl accuse the reverend of?

a Having no respect for authority

b Bearing shame in his heart

c Being caught by the Black Man

---

1 그렇지 않으면 악마가 이미 목사님을 붙잡은 것처럼 엄마도 붙잡을 거예요.

2 헤스터 프린이 가슴에 저 글자를 달고 치욕을 견디는 것이 마음속에 그것을 숨기고 사는 것보다 덜 비참하다고 생각하세요? → rather than…: ~라기 보다

3 제게 말하지 못한 어떤 비밀이 있는지 알고 싶습니다. → if: ~인지 아닌지

This probing line of questioning visibly flustered the reverend. "But. . . of course I have," he stammered. "Of course there are parts of my soul I could never expose to an Earthly doctor."

"But how can I cure your body if you have not laid open your mind and soul?"[1]

At this, the reverend suddenly became fiercely angry and shoved the doctor's hands away from him. With a frantic gesture, he stormed out of the room.

Within a couple of hours, the reverend returned to the doctor's laboratory and apologized for his outburst. The two resumed their friendship effortlessly. But later that day, while the reverend slept in his chair, the doctor crept silently into his room. Putting his hand on the sleeping man's chest, the doctor pushed back the reverend's shirt and looked at his bare chest.[2] The doctor shuddered for a moment at

☐ probe （진상을) 규명하다, 탐구하다
☐ visibly 눈에 보이게, 뚜렷하게
☐ fluster 어리둥절하게 하다, 당황하게 하다
☐ stammer 말을 더듬다
☐ expose to ~에 드러내다
☐ cure 치료하다, 치료
☐ lay open 폭로하다, 드러내다 (lay-laid-laid)
☐ fiercely 사납게
☐ shove （난폭하게） 밀다
☐ frantic 광란의, 미친 사람 같은
☐ storm 돌격하다, 돌진하다
☐ apologize for ~에 대해 사과하다
☐ outburst （격정 등의） 폭발
☐ resume 재개하다, 다시 시작하다
☐ effortlessly 힘들이지 않고, 쉽게
☐ creep 살금살금 걷다; 슬며시 퍼지다
☐ bare 발가벗은, 살을 드러낸
☐ devilish 악마 같은, 흉악한
☐ subtly 미묘하게
☐ maintain 유지하다

what he saw. Then a devilish look of happiness and satisfaction crept across his face.

After this day, the relationship between Roger Chillingworth and Reverend Arthur Dimmesdale changed subtly. The doctor maintained his calm appearance. But secretly, he was controlling the reverend and planning to take revenge on him.[3]

✔ Check Up

Why did the doctor change his attitude toward the reverend?

- a He saw something on the reverend's skin.
- b He felt pity for the reverend because of his illness.
- c He respected the reverend's desire to keep his secret.

1 하지만 당신의 마음과 영혼을 드러내지 않으면 제가 어떻게 당신의 육신을 치료할 수 있겠습니까?

2 의사는 잠자는 목사의 가슴에 손을 얹어 목사의 셔츠를 뒤로 제치고는 그의 맨 가슴을 보았다.

3 그러나 그는 비밀스럽게 목사를 통제하면서 그에 대한 복수를 계획하고 있었다.
   → take [get] revenge on: ~에게 복수하다

Dimmesdale often punished himself secretly for the crime he had committed. He would force himself to go without food and sleep, and would even whip himself until he was bloody.[1] Then one night he thought of a new method for self-punishment. In the middle of the night, he got dressed and quietly left the house.

As if he were walking through a dream, the reverend went to the western end of the marketplace, to the scaffolding where Hester Prynne had stood seven years earlier.[2]

On that dark May night, the reverend climbed the steps of the scaffolding and stood on the platform atop it. He felt that the town was asleep and that there was no danger of anyone discovering him.

But while he stood there, his mind was overcome with horror, and he felt the scarlet letter burning from within his breast. It was the source of his pain and illness. Then suddenly, he released a shriek so long and loud that he expected the whole town to awake and come running to see him in his place of shame.[3]

But the drowsy townspeople must have thought his voice was merely the cries of wild animals or the cackles of witches, because nobody came running.[4]

---

[1] 그는 음식도 잠도 없이 지내도록 스스로를 몰아붙이기도 하고, 심지어 피투성이가 되도록 자신을 채찍질하기도 했다. → would: ~하곤 했다 (과거의 반복적인 행위를 나타냄.)

[2] 마치 꿈속을 걷는 것처럼 목사는 시장의 서쪽 끝, 헤스터 프린이 7년 전에 서 있었던 처형대로 갔다.

[3] 그러다 갑자기 아주 길게 큰 소리로 비명을 지르는 바람에 그는 마을 전체가 잠에서 깨어나 그의 수치스러운 모습을 보러 달려올 거라고 생각했다.

[4] 그러나 잠에 취한 마을 사람들은 그의 목소리를 그저 야생동물의 울음소리나 마녀들이 깔깔거리는 소리라고 생각한 것 같았다. 왜냐하면 아무도 달려오지 않았기 때문이다.

Then the reverend perceived a light approaching from the distance. When it got close enough for him to recognize the bearer, the reverend saw that it was Pastor Wilson.[1] The pastor did not notice the reverend and kept walking past. The reverend knew that the pastor was coming from a late night vigil in the death chamber of Governor Winthrop, who had probably just passed away.

After the pastor passed, another light approached. This time the reverend could see that it was Hester Prynne and Pearl.

"Hester Prynne," said the reverend, "is that you?"

"Reverend Dimmesdale," exclaimed Hester, who was taken by surprise to find him standing atop the scaffolding in the dark.[2] "Yes, it is Pearl and I. We are coming from Governor Winthrop's death chamber, where I measured him for a robe. We're on the way back to our cottage."

□ from the distance 멀리서	□ measure ~의 치수를 재다
□ get close 가까워지다	□ robe 예복, 관복; 길고 헐거운 겉옷
□ bearer 운반인	□ on the way to ~로 가는 도중에
□ notice 알아채다	□ fresh 신선한
□ vigil 철야, 불침번	□ pour into 흘러 들어오다
□ death chamber 임종실; 사형실	□ rush 돌진하다
□ pass away 죽다, 사망하다	□ vein 정맥, 혈관
□ exclaim 외치다	□ weight 무게; 부담, 책임
□ take A by surprise A를 놀라게 하다	□ lift 들어올리다

"Hester, Pearl, come up here," said the reverend. "You have both been up here before, but I was not with you."

Silently, Hester held Pearl's hand, and they climbed up the steps of the platform. In the darkness, the reverend found Pearl's hand and held it. A fresh force of life poured into his heart, and the blood rushed through his veins.[3] The weight was lifted from his soul!

1 등불을 든 사람을 알아볼 수 있을 정도로 불빛이 가까워졌을 때, 목사는 그 사람이 윌슨 목사임을 알았다.

2 "딤스데일 목사님." 헤스터는 어둠 속에서 처형대 위에 서 있는 그를 발견하고는 깜짝 놀라서 외쳤다.

3 신선한 생명의 힘이 그의 가슴으로 밀려 들어왔고 혈관으로 피가 빠르게 흘렀다.

"Reverend," said little Pearl, "will you stand here tomorrow at noon with me and my mother?"

"No, not tomorrow," said the reverend. "But I shall one day."

"But when?" asked Pearl.

"I shall stand with you and your mother before the Lord on Judgment Day," he answered.

☐ meteor 유성, 운석
☐ light up 비추다 (light-lit-lit)
☐ luminescence 발광
☐ frightened of ~이 겁나는
☐ hate 증오하다
☐ lip 입술
☐ nonsense 허튼 소리, 터무니없는 소리
☐ mock 조롱하다, 비웃다

1 그 광채 속에 주홍글씨 A를 가슴에 단 헤스터, 자신의 가슴에 손을 얹은 목사, 그리고 두 사람의 손을 잡은 펄이 서 있었다. → 부사구가 문장 앞에 온 도치문.

2 목사가 다시 눈길을 지상으로 돌렸을 때, 펄이 멀리서 다가오고 있는 한 사람을 가리키고 있는 것을 보았다.

Pearl laughed at this, and suddenly a meteor flashed and lit up the night sky. There in its luminescence stood Hester with her scarlet A, the reverend, holding his hand over his heart, and Pearl, holding both their hands.[1]

When he returned his eyes to earth, the reverend saw Pearl pointing toward a person coming closer from the distance.[2] As the person came closer, they saw that it was Roger Chillingworth.

"Hester, who is that man?" asked the reverend. "I've become frightened of him. I've started to hate him!"

"I can tell you who he is," said Pearl. Then she put her lips to the reverend's ear and whispered nonsense, and then she laughed out loud.[3]

"Child, are you mocking me?" asked the reverend.

"You are not true," said the little girl. "You won't stand here with me and mother tomorrow at noon!"

✔ *Check Up*

본문의 내용과 일치하면 T, 일치하지 않으면 F를 쓰세요.

a) Pearl thinks that Judgmert Day will be tomorrow at noon.　____
b) The reverend was delighted to see Roger coming toward them.　____

정답: a. T b. F

3　그러더니 그 아이는 자신의 입술을 목사의 귀에 대고 터무니없는 말을 속삭이고는 큰 소리로 웃었다.

"Good sir," said Roger Chillingworth, who had come up to the scaffolding. "What ever are you doing out here at this time of night? Have you been sleep-walking?"

"How did you know I was here?" asked the reverend fearfully.

"I had no idea you were here. I was just walking home from the governor's death chamber. You'd better come home with me now, or you'll not have enough energy to give your sermon tomorrow."[1]

"Yes," said the reverend, "I'll go home with you." The man suddenly felt cold and depressed, as if rudely awaken from a dream.

After the night on the scaffolding, Hester Prynne became worried that the reverend was losing his mind. She remembered her agreement with Roger Chillingworth some years earlier, that she would hide

---

his true identity as her husband.[2]

But now she felt it was her fault for not warning the reverend of Chillingworth's terrible inten- tions. She resolved that she would speak with Chillingworth and tell him that she could no longer keep that promise.[3] She had to tell the reverend who his tormentor really was.

Hester did not have to wait long to speak with the doctor. She saw him in the forest, gathering plants one afternoon a few days later.

"Run along, and play," she said to Pearl, "I want to speak with the doctor." Then she turned to Chillingworth and said, "Doctor, I need to speak with you about an important matter."

---

1 지금 저와 함께 집으로 가는 게 좋을 것 같군요. 그렇지 않으면 내일 설교할 힘이 충분히 없을 겁니다. → or: 그렇지 않으면

2 그녀는 몇 년 전 자신의 남편이라는 그의 진짜 정체를 숨겨 주기로 한 로저 칠링워스와의 합의를 기억했다.

3 그녀는 칠링워스와 얘기해서 그에게 더 이상 그 약속을 지킬 수 없다고 말하기로 결심했다.

"Ah, Mistress Hester," he said with a smile, "I hear
the town council may soon allow you to take that
scarlet letter off your bosom."

□ mistress 주부, 여주인
□ council 평의회, 자문회
□ be worthy to부정사 ~할 가치가 있다
□ fall off 떨어지다
□ by oneself 스스로, 혼자서
□ transform 변형시키다
□ creature 창조물, 생물, 사람

□ resemble 닮다
□ devil 악마
□ seek 추구하다, 구하다
  (seek-sought-sought)
□ seriously 진지하게, 엄숙하게
□ weep 눈물을 흘리다, 울다
  (weep-wept-wept)

1 제가 그걸 끝낼 만한 가치가 있는 사람이라면, 그것은 저절로 떨어질 거예요.
  → be done with: ~이 끝나다

"If I were worthy to be done with it, it would fall off by itself,"[1] she replied, noticing that the past seven years had transformed Chillingworth into a creature that resembled a devil. She knew that his life of seeking revenge must have been transforming his mind, body, and soul into such a dark form.[2]

"What do you see in my face that makes you look at it so seriously?" asked the doctor.

"Something that makes me want to weep," she answered. "But let us speak of another miserable man. Seven years ago, I promised to keep your identity a secret. But I have a duty to help this man who you are slowly killing. I must tell him who you are so that he may understand why you are tormenting him."[3]

✔ Check Up

What did Hester want to do?

a She wanted to tell the townspeople who Pearl's father was.

b She wanted to tell everyone that she was married to the doctor.

c She wanted to tell Reverend Dimmesdale who the doctor really was.

---

2 그녀는 복수를 추구하는 삶이 그의 몸과 마음과 영혼을 그렇게 어두운 모습으로 변하게 만든 게 틀림없음을 알았다. → must have + 과거분사: ~했음에 틀림없다

3 저는 그에게 당신이 누구인지 얘기해야 돼요. 그래야 그가 왜 당신이 괴롭히는지 이해할 테니까요. → so that...: ~하기 위해서

"That cowardly priest is conscious of my influence and my curse," said Chillingworth. "He's just too afraid to admit it to himself. You are foolish to want to help such a low wretch as him, who abandoned you with child to the mercy of this town for all these years."[1]

"I must help him," cried Hester. "This scarlet letter instructs me to do so. I will keep your secret no longer."

"Go ahead, and tell him," said Chillingworth. "I pity you for wasting your goodness on that weak shamble of a man."

"I pity you, too," Hester answered. "I pity you for suffering such hatred that it has changed a wise man into a demon!"[2]

□ priest 성직자, 사제
□ be conscious of ~을 의식하고 있다, 깨닫고 있다
□ curse 저주, 악담; 저주하다
□ admit 인정하다
□ wretch 철면피, 비열한 사람
□ abandon 버리다, 포기하다
□ instruct A to부정사 A에게 ~하라고 지시하다

□ waste 낭비하다; 저하시키다
□ goodness 선량함, 착함
□ shamble 휘청거림, 비틀거림
□ hatred 증오
□ arrange 배열하다
□ meaning 의미
□ be doomed to부정사 <보통 부정적으로> ~할 운명이 되다

Hester found Pearl down by the stream where she had been playing. The little girl had arranged a green A, just like her mother's, on the bosom of her dress.[3]

"Ah, my Pearl, but your green A does not have the same meaning as the one I'm doomed to wear. Do you know why I wear this letter?"

"I do," answered Pearl. "For the same reason that the reverend holds his hand over his heart."[4]

✔ *Check Up*

빈칸에 들어갈 알맞은 말을 본문에서 찾아 쓰세요.

If you want to ____________ a secret,
you should tell no one about it.

정답 : keep

---

1 그 세월 동안 당신을 아이와 함께 이 마을에 내맡긴 그런 저급하고 비열한 사람을 돕고 싶어 하다니 어리석구려. → to the mercy of: ~이 하라는 대로

2 현명한 사람을 악마로 바꿔 버린 그런 증오심으로 고통받다니 당신이 불쌍해요!

3 어린 소녀는 자신의 드레스 가슴 위에 엄마의 것과 똑같이 녹색의 A자를 배열했다.

4 목사님이 자신의 가슴에 손을 얹고 있는 것과 같은 이유 때문이에요.

Comprehension Quiz

A 다음 중 옳은 설명은 **T**, 틀린 설명은 **F**에 표시하세요.

1. Pearl was a very normal little girl. T F

2. Hester Prynne wanted the town to take Pearl away from her. T F

3. Pearl could not be forced to adapt to rules. T F

4. Hester Prynne told Pearl they were going to the governor's mansion to return a pair of gloves the governor had asked her to embroider. T F

5. Pearl could not accept her position as an outcast in the town. T F

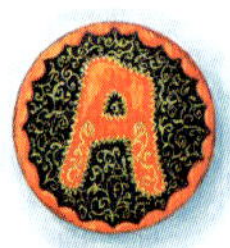

B 다음 중 본문의 내용상 밑줄 친 표현이 올바르게 쓰인 것을 고르세요.

1. (a) The two men soon became constant <u>companions</u>.

   (b) He used plants from the forest to make <u>companions</u>.

2. (a) He pushed aside the man's hands <u>effortlessly</u>.

   (b) The two resumed their friendship <u>effortlessly</u>.

3. (a) The doctor <u>shuddered</u> for a moment at what he saw.

   (b) The <u>shuddered</u> leaves were ugly.

Answers

A ① F ② F ③ T ④ T ⑤ F
B ① (a) ② (b) ③ (a)

C 다음 질문에 맞는 답을 고르세요.

1 Where did Pearl tell the governor and Pastor Wilson she came from?

(a) She told them she came from Heaven.

(b) She told them she came from her mother.

(c) She told them she came from the rosebush on the side of the prison.

2 Why did Chillingworth suggest they study Pearl's nature?

(a) To guess the identity of her father.

(b) Because she was so strange.

(c) To determine if she was a demon child from Hell.

3 Where did Roger Chillingworth say the ugly leaves had grown from?

(a) From the nose of the Black Man.

(b) From the heart of a man buried with a secret sin.

(c) From the rosebush growing on the side of the prison.

4 Why did Reverend Dimmesdale climb to the top of the scaffolding at night?

(a) Because he wanted to punish himself for a sin.

(b) Because he wanted to see the far side of the town.

(c) Because he wanted to enjoy a beautiful summer night.

Answers

C   **1** (c)   **2** (a)   **3** (b)   **4** (a)

Hester remained strong in her resolve to tell the reverend just who Roger Chillingworth really was. On a day Hester knew that the reverend would be passing through the forest, she set out to cross his path, taking along little Pearl.[1] As they entered the forest, Pearl cried out, "Mother, the sunshine doesn't love you! It runs away and hides because of the A on your bosom!"

"Then you had better run away and try to catch it!" answered her mother. The little girl actually did catch the sun, standing amid its brilliant splendor.

☐ **set out** 출발하다, 길을 떠나다
☐ **cross one's path** ~와 우연히 만나다
☐ **actually** 사실, 실제로
☐ **brilliant** 찬란한
☐ **splendor** 훌륭함; 빛남, 광채
☐ **rest** 쉬다
☐ **for a while** 잠시 동안
☐ **clasp** 걸쇠, 죔쇠

1 어느 날 헤스터는 목사가 숲속을 지나갈 거라는 걸 알고, 그와 우연히 만나기 위해 어린 펄을 데리고 집을 나섰다.

2 철로 된 걸쇠가 달린 커다랗고 무거운 검은 책을 들고 숲에 나타나는 악마에 대한 얘기요.

As they passed deeper into the forest, Pearl asked her mother to sit and rest for a while.

"Tell me a story," she demanded.

"A story about what?" asked Hester.

"A story about the Black Man who haunts the forest with his big, heavy, black book with iron clasps.[2] And tell me about how he makes people write their names in his book using their own blood! Did you ever meet the Black Man, Mother?"

Then you **had better run away** and try to catch it!
그러면 네가 뛰어가서 잡아 오는 게 좋겠구나!

had better + 동사원형: ~하는 게 낫다 → 경고의 의미로 윗사람에게는 쓰지 않는 게 좋다.

ex. You **had better finish** your work before going to bed.
자기 전에 일부터 끝내는 게 좋을 걸세.

"Who told you about this?" Hester asked.

"Last night, when we were at the house you were watching, the old woman thought I was asleep while she spoke of it.[1] She said that the scarlet letter was the Black Man's mark on you."

"I'll tell you a story about the Black Man if you won't ask me any more afterward," said Hester. "I met the Black Man once, and this scarlet letter is his mark."

Suddenly, Hester heard footsteps coming through the forest.

"Pearl, run along now, and play. I want to speak with the man who's coming toward us."[2]

"Is it the Black Man?" inquired Pearl.

"Of course not, silly child. It is the reverend."

"It is," said Pearl, who could now see the reverend coming through the darkened forest. "And he has his hand over his heart. That's because he wrote his name in the book and the Black Man put his mark

□ asleep 잠이 든
□ afterward 이후에
□ footstep 발소리; 걸음
□ inquire 묻다, 질문하다
□ silly 어리석은, 지각 없는
□ darkened 어두워진
□ on the outside 바깥에
□ stream 시내, 개울

over the reverend's heart.[3] But why doesn't he wear
it on the outside like you?"

"Now, go, child!" cried Hester. "Stay near the
stream, and don't go too far!"

Pearl walked away, singing to herself. Hester saw
the reverend coming down the path. He looked
weaker and more depressed than ever.

---

1 어젯밤 엄마가 지키고 있던 그 집에 우리가 있을 때, 할머니가 제가 잠든 줄 알고 그 얘기를 했
   어요.

2 나는 우리 쪽으로 걸어오는 저 분과 얘기를 나누고 싶구나.

3 그건 목사님이 그 명부에 자신의 이름을 썼고, 악마가 목사님의 가슴에 낙인을 찍었기 때문이
   에요. → That's because...: 그것은 ~때문이다

"Arthur Dimmesdale," she called out to him. "Reverend Dimmesdale!"

"Who speaks?" answered the reverend nervously. "Hester, is that you?"

"Yes, it is I," she answered. They had not been alone together in over seven years because of their situation.[1] They were both nervous and happy to see one another.

<table>
<tr><td>☐ call out to ~를 소리쳐 부르다</td><td>☐ purity 청렴; 청순, 순수</td></tr>
<tr><td>☐ nervously 초조하게, 신경질적으로</td><td>☐ follower 신봉자, 신도</td></tr>
<tr><td>☐ fix 고정시키다</td><td>☐ emptiness 공허함</td></tr>
<tr><td>☐ drearily 쓸쓸하게, 음울하게</td><td>☐ agony 고통</td></tr>
<tr><td>☐ symbol 상징</td><td>☐ torture 고문하다</td></tr>
<tr><td>☐ nothing but 오직 (= only)</td><td>☐ repent 후회하다, 뉘우치다</td></tr>
<tr><td>☐ despair 절망</td><td>☐ holy 성스러운</td></tr>
<tr><td>☐ preach 설교하다</td><td>☐ garment 의복</td></tr>
</table>

Fixing his eyes on her, he asked, "Hester, have you found peace?"

She smiled drearily and looked down at the symbol on her bosom. "Have you?"

"No, I have found nothing but darkness and despair! I preach purity to my followers, but I know the emptiness and agony of what I truly am.[2] I feel like Satan is always laughing at me."

"You are wrong to torture yourself like this," said Hester. "You have repented deeply for years now. You must learn to leave your sin in the past!"

"No, Hester," cried the reverend. "I'm not worthy to wear these holy garments that clothe me.[3] You are lucky to wear the A on your chest. My mark burns within me! If only I had one friend to whom I could tell the truth of my sins!"[4]

✔ Check Up

본문의 내용과 일치하면 T, 일치하지 않으면 F를 쓰세요.

a The reverend is in agony because he knows he is a hypocrite. _____

b Hester and Dimmesdale met together by themselves often. _____

정답: a. T b. F

1 그들은 자신들의 상황 때문에 7년 이상 단둘이 있지 못했다.

2 나는 신도들에게 청렴을 설교하지만, 내 존재의 공허함과 고뇌를 알고 있소.

3 나는 나를 감싸고 있는 이런 성스러운 옷을 입을 가치가 없소.

4 내 죄의 진상을 털어놓을 수 있는 친구가 한 사람만 있다면! → if only...: ~하기만 하면

"I am that friend and your partner in sin," said Hester. Then she struggled to give the reverend the message that was the reason for their meeting on this day.[1] "You also have a great enemy, who lives under the same roof as you."

"An enemy under my roof?" the reverend said with surprise. "What do you mean?"

"Oh Arthur," cried Hester. "Please forgive me. A long time ago, I agreed to deceive you. The old man, the doctor whom they call Roger Chillingworth, he was my husband!"

A look of terrible violence came over the reverend's face. He sank down to the ground and buried his face in his hands.

"I should have known it!" groaned the reverend. "My heart told me he was hiding a terrible secret from the day I first met him.[2] Why did I not understand? Oh, Hester Prynne! You are responsible for

---

☐ **struggle to**부정사 ~하려고 애쓰다, 고심하다
☐ **message** 용건; 메시지
☐ **enemy** 적, 원수
☐ **roof** 지붕
☐ **forgive** 용서하다
☐ **agree to**부정사 ~하는 데 동의하다
☐ **deceive** 속이다

☐ **violence** 격렬, 사나움; 폭력
☐ **sink down** 맥없이 주저앉다 (sink-sank-sunk)
☐ **groan** 신음하다
☐ **throw one's arms around** 양팔로 ~를 껴안다 (throw-threw-thrown)
☐ **rest on** ~에 얹혀져 있다, ~에 기대다
☐ **over and over** 거듭해서, 몇 번이고

this! I can never forgive you!" he shouted.

Hester Prynne threw her arms around the reverend and held him close to her. His cheek rested on the scarlet letter. He tried to struggle free, but she would not let him go.[3]

"You must forgive me," she said over and over. "You must forgive me."

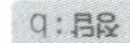

✔ *Check Up*

Why was the reverend angry at Hester?

☐ a She was a married woman.

☐ b He blamed her for his situation.

☐ c She would not forgive him.

정답: b

---

1 그런 다음 그녀는 이날 그들이 만나는 이유인 용건을 목사에게 전하려고 애썼다.

2 그를 처음 만난 날부터 내 마음은 그가 끔찍한 비밀을 숨기고 있다고 내게 얘기하고 있었소.

3 그는 벗어나려고 했지만, 그녀는 그를 놓아 주려 하지 않았다. → let A go: A를 놓아 주다, 가게 하다

"Yes," cried the reverend softly. "I forgive you now. We are not the worst sinners in the world. That old man's revenge is blacker than my sin. He is killing me in cold blood. What we did was not so bad as that."

- □ in cold blood 냉혹하게, 냉정하게
- □ sacredness 신성함
- □ make love 사랑을 나누다
- □ gloomy 어두운, 음침한; 우울한
- □ charm 매력; 마력, 마법
- □ linger (아쉬운 듯) 남아 있다, 꾸물거리다
- □ reveal 드러내다, 밝히다
- □ point one's finger at ~를 손가락질하다
- □ satisfy 만족시키다
- □ passion 열정
- □ get away from ~에서 달아나다
- □ hysterically 발작적으로

1 맞아요. 우리가 한 일에는 나름대로 신성함이 있었어요.

2 하지만 그 어둠 속에는 그들을 함께 머물러 있게 만드는 마력이 있었다.

3 그는 복수에 대한 자신의 어두운 열정을 만족시킬 만한 다른 비밀스러운 방법들을 찾아낼 거예요.

"No, what we did had a sacredness of its own.[1] We told that to each other when we made love," she whispered. "Have you forgotten?"

"No," he whispered. "I have not forgotten."

This was the gloomiest hour of their lives. But in the darkness of it, there was a charm that made them linger together.[2] There they sat amid the dark forest, holding hands and kissing.

"Roger Chillingworth knows that you will reveal his identity," said the reverend. "Now he will point his finger at me in front of the whole town."

"No, I don't think he'll reveal your sin to the public," she said. "He will find other secret ways to satisfy his dark passion for revenge.[3] You must get away from this terrible man!"

"Yes, he's killing me," cried the reverend hysterically. "But what can I do, Hester? Help me, please!"

One Point

What we did was **not so bad as** that.
우리가 저지른 일은 그렇게 나쁜 일은 아니었소.

not so + 형용사의 원급 + as: ~만큼 …하지 않다
ex. She is **not so beautiful as** her sister. 그녀는 여동생만큼 예쁘지는 않다.

"The sea brought you to this New World, and it can carry you back to the old one.[1] You should go back to England, or you could live in Germany, France, or even in Italy."

"But how could I leave my post here? Even though my soul is ruined, I'm needed to help others."

"You can't help anybody if you're crushed under the weight of your misery.[2] You must leave this place behind," she said. "The future could be filled with new chances for success. Do anything except lay down and die!"

"Oh, Hester," cried the reverend. "I must die here. I don't have the strength or courage to risk going back into the strange, cold world alone."[3]

Then in a deep whisper, Hester replied, "You will not go alone."

At this, Arthur Dimmesdale looked into her eyes with joy and hope.

☐ post 지위, 직
☐ even though... 비록 ~이지만
☐ ruined 파멸한; 타락한
☐ crush 눌러 부수다, 뭉개다
☐ misery 고통, 비참(함), 불행
☐ be filled with ~으로 가득 차다
☐ success 성공

☐ strength 힘
☐ courage 용기
☐ risk + 동명사 감행하다, 감히 ~하다
☐ unhook 갈고리에서 벗기다
☐ fling away (세차게) 던져 버리다
☐ glitter 반짝반짝 빛나다
☐ jewel 보석

"We won't look back," said Hester. "The past is gone. See!"

Then with her fingers she unhooked the scarlet letter from her breast and flung it away from her onto a rock at the edge of the stream.[4] The letter lay there, glittering like a lost jewel.

1 바다가 당신을 이 신세계로 데려왔으니, 그것은 당신을 다시 구세계로 데려갈 수 있을 거예요.
   → the old one = the Old World (유럽을 의미함)

2 만약 당신이 고통의 무게에 짓눌려 망가진다면 당신은 누구도 도울 수 없어요.

3 그 낯설고 냉혹한 세계로 감히 혼자 돌아갈 만한 힘이나 용기가 내게는 없소.

4 그런 다음 그녀는 손가락으로 자기 가슴에서 주홍글씨를 떼어내더니, 그것을 개울가에 있는 바위 위로 세차게 던져 버렸다.

Hester heaved a huge sigh of relief as the burden of shame and anguish left her heart. The freedom she felt made her realize what a weight it had truly been.[1] Hester undid her cap and let her dark, beautiful hair fall down around her shoulders.[2] Then the sunlight came through the tops of the trees and flooded the forest.

Hester looked again at the reverend with eyes full of joy and said, "Now you must get to know our little Pearl! You have seen her, but you do not really know her yet![3] She's a strange child, but you will learn to love her dearly."

"Do you think she will want to know me?" asked the reverend hopefully, "I have always been afraid of little Pearl."

□ **heave a sigh** 한숨 쉬다
□ **relief** 안도 *v.* relieve
□ **burden** 짐
□ **anguish** 격통, 고뇌
□ **freedom** 자유
□ **realize** 깨닫다
□ **undo** (의복 등을) 벗다; 원상태로 되돌리다
□ **flood** (홍수처럼) 와락 쏟아져 들어오다
□ **get to know** 알게 되다
□ **dearly** 깊이, 극진히
□ **gather up** 모으다
□ **obey** 복종하다, 따르다
□ **devoid of** ~이 없는
□ **stamp** 발을 구르다

1 그녀가 느끼는 자유는 그 글자의 무게가 실제로 어떠했는지를 깨닫게 해주었다.

2 헤스터는 모자를 벗고 자신의 검고 아름다운 머리가 어깨에 흘러내리게 내버려 두었다.

"Ah, that is so sad," answered Hester. "She will love you dearly. She is not far off now. I will call her. Pearl! Pearl!"

Pearl was away, gathering up flowers for her mother. She heard the call and came back toward them slowly.

"Come here," said Hester. "I want you to become a dear friend of the reverend."

But Pearl did not obey her mother's command. The child only pointed to her mother's breast, devoid of the scarlet letter, and stamped her foot.[4]

본문의 내용과 일치하면 T, 일치하지 않으면 F를 쓰세요.

[a] Hester regretted throwing the scarlet letter away. ____
[b] Hester wanted Dimmesdale to teach Pearl how to behave herself. ____

정답 : a F b F

3 당신은 그 아이를 보아왔지만, 사실 아직은 그 아이를 잘 몰라요!

4 그 아이는 주홍글씨가 사라진 엄마의 가슴을 가리키며 발을 구를 뿐이었다.

"I see," said Hester. "Small children don't like to see the things they've always known change even slightly.[1] She is missing the letter that she's seen on me since the day she was born." Hester pointed to the letter at the edge of the stream and said, "There's the letter, Pearl. Bring it to me now."

"You pick it up yourself," replied Pearl.

Frustrated with the child, Hester sighed and walked to the side of the stream and hooked the letter back on her breast.

"Do you know your mother now, child?" she said to her daughter.

"Yes, now you are my mother indeed!" said little Pearl, bounding across the stream to join them.

"Come and see him, Pearl. He wants to greet you. He loves you. Will you love him, too?" asked Hester.

"Does he really love us?" Pearl asked, looking at her mother in the eyes with sharp intelligence. "Will he walk hand in hand with us into town?"

☐ slightly 약간
☐ frustrated 좌절하여, 실망하여
☐ hook 갈고리에 걸다
☐ bound 뛰다, 기운차게 걷다
☐ join 합류하다, 참가하다
☐ greet 인사하다; 맞이하다
☐ sharp 날카로운

☐ hand in hand 손을 맞잡고
☐ all the time 항상, 늘
☐ embarrassed 당황한
☐ stoop over ~위로 몸을 굽히다
☐ soften (마음을) 누그러지게 하다
☐ brow 눈썹; 이마
☐ apart from ~에서 떨어진

"Not now, child," answered Hester. "But soon he will be with us all the time."

"And will he always keep his hand over his heart?" Pearl inquired.

Dimmesdale, embarrassed by the child's questions, stooped over and kissed her forehead, hoping to soften her view of him.[2] But as soon as his lips left her forehead, she ran to the stream and washed the kiss off her brow, as if it were something dirty.[3] Then she stayed apart from her mother and the reverend while they discussed their plans to be together in the near future.

Which is the best word to describe Pearl?

a Spoiled

b Dutiful

c Respectful

정답 : a

---

1 어린 아이들은 자신이 늘 알고 있던 것들이 조금이라도 바뀌는 걸 보고 싶어 하지 않아요.

2 아이의 질문들에 당황한 딤스데일은 자신에 대한 아이의 생각이 누그러지길 바라며 아이에게 몸을 굽히고 이마에 입을 맞췄다.

3 하지만 그의 입술이 이마를 떠나자마자, 아이는 개울로 달려가 마치 더러운 것이라도 되는 양 이마에서 그 키스 자국을 씻어냈다.

문학작품에서 상징은 중요한 역할을 합니다. 호손 또한 《주홍글씨》에 여러 상징들을 심어 놓았는데요, 이에 대해 좀더 자세히 살펴봅시다.

The Symbols in the Scarlet Letter

《주홍글씨》 안의 상징들

Hawthorne used symbols throughout the "Scarlet Letter" to reinforce his main ideas. The most important symbol in the "Scarlet Letter" is, of course, the red letter "A" itself. This letter stands for "adultery" and is an obvious symbol of Hester's sin. However, Hester wears it proudly, and it changes meanings as time passes. Eventually, it can be seen as a symbol for "able". Pearl, Hester's daughter, serves as a symbol of a living version of the scarlet letter. She is troublesome, and this punishes Hester. On the other hand, she is also a blessing. Pearl gives her mother reason to live.

reinforce 보강하다   stand for 상징하다   obvious 명백한   meaning 의미   troublesome 성가신, 귀찮은
punish 벌하다   punishment 처벌   give in 굴복하다, 따르다   demand 요구   meteor 유성
Judgement Day 심판의 날   literary 문학의

호손은 《주홍글씨》 전반에 그의 주제를 강조하기 위해 상징들을 사용했습니다. 《주홍글씨》에서 가장 중요한 상징은 물론 빨간 색 글씨 A입니다. 이 글씨는 '간음'을 상징하며 헤스터의 죄에 대한 명백한 상징이죠. 하지만 헤스터는 이것을 자랑스레 달고 다녔고, 시간이 흐르면서 의미가 바뀌게 됩니다. 결국 그것은 '유능함'의 상징으로 보입니다. 헤스터의 딸, 펄은 주홍글씨의 살아 있는 상징 역할을 합니다. 그 아이는 말썽꾸러기여서, 이 때문에 헤스터가 혼이 나죠. 한편 이 꼬마는 은총이기도 합니다. 펄은 그녀의 어머니에게 살아갈 이유를 주거든요.

Compared to Pearl, the scarlet letter is almost useless because Pearl is a symbol of the passion that created the sin. This reflects the uselessness of the Puritan "punishment" that is given to Hester. Hester would not give in to their demands, and instead becomes a proud and independent woman.

Another symbol appears in the form of the meteor that lights up the night sky as Dimmesdale stands on the scaffolding with Hester and Pearl. Just after he tells Pearl he will stand with her mother on Judgment Day, this light from this meteor "reveals" to the world that Dimmesdale belongs with Hester and Pearl. We find out later that he is actually Pearl's father. These types of symbols are literary techniques that authors use to help reinforce their main themes.

펄과 견주어 보면 주홍글씨는 별 소용이 없습니다. 펄은 죄를 낳은 정욕의 상징이기 때문입니다. 이 점은 청교도들이 헤스터에게 내린 처벌이 소용 없음을 보여줍니다. 헤스터는 그들의 요구에 굴하지 않으려 했고, 자부심 강한 독립적인 여성이 되었습니다.

또 하나의 상징은 유성의 형태로 나타납니다. 딤스데일이 헤스터와 펄과 함께 처형대에 서 있는 동안 밤하늘을 밝힌 그 유성 말입니다. 그 목사가 펄에게 심판의 날에 그녀의 어머니와 함께 처형대에 서겠다고 말한 직후, 이 유성에서 나온 빛은 딤스데일이 헤스터, 펄과 관련이 있음을 세상에 드러냅니다. 우리는 나중에 그가 실제로 펄의 아버지라는 것을 알게 되죠. 이런 유형의 상징들은 작가들이 자신의 주제를 보강하기 위해 사용하는 문학적 기법입니다.

CHAPTER FIVE

The Revelation

After leaving the forest, the reverend could not believe their meeting had been real. They had decided that the cities of Europe would be the best place for them to begin their new lives. And it happened that there was a ship in Boston Harbor set to leave for the Old World in four days. Through Hester's charity work, she knew the ship's captain and was able to make arrangements that she, the reverend, and Pearl would depart with the ship.[1]

When Hester told the reverend of her arrangement, he was overjoyed and remarked, "How fortunate, as I'm set to give the election sermon in only three day's time."

□ revelation 폭로, 누설	□ commemorate 기념하다, 축하하다
□ harbor 항구	□ swearing-in 취임(식)
□ leave for ~로 떠나다	□ high point 절정
□ depart 출발하다	□ career 경력
□ be overjoyed 아주 기뻐하다	□ possess 소유하다, 지니다
□ fortunate 행운의, 운이 좋은	□ a sense of ~감, 기분
□ election 선거, 당선	□ unusual 보통이 아닌

1 자선활동을 통해 헤스터는 그 배의 선장을 알게 되었고, 자신과 목사와 펄이 그 배로 떠나도록 준비할 수 있었다. → make an arrangement: 준비를 하다

The election sermon, to commemorate the swearing-in of the new governor, was the high point in the career of any New England clergyman.[2]

Dimmesdale returned from his talk with Hester possessing a sense of great physical energy that was very unusual for him. He found that no matter what he did, he could not become tired.

[2] 새 주지사의 취임을 축하하기 위한 당선 설교는 뉴잉글랜드 성직자의 경력에 절정이 되는 것이었다.

He found that **no matter what** he did, he could not become tired.
그는 자신이 무슨 일을 하더라도 지칠 수 없다는 걸 알게 됐다.

no matter what: 아무리 무엇을 ~하더라도 (= whatever)
ex. **No matter what** I say, he will not believe me.
　　내가 무슨 말을 하더라도, 그는 믿지 않을 거야.

Finally, the reverend entered the peace and solitude of his study, where he could write his most important election sermon. While he was occupied with this task, there came a knock on the door. When the reverend said, "Come in," he feared he would behold an evil spirit, and he did.[1] It was Roger Chillingworth. The reverend remained speechless.

□ solitude 고독
□ be occupied with ~에 몰두하다
□ task 일, 직무, 과업
□ fear 두려워하다
□ behold 주시하다, 보다
□ speechless 말문이 막힌, 말 못하는
□ suspect ~이 아닐까 생각하다

□ assistance 도움, 원조
□ solemnly 숙연히, 진지하게
□ provide A with B A에게 B를 제공하다
□ renewal 갱신, 회복
□ trusted 믿을 만한
□ Heaven grant it... 제발 ~이기를
□ frame 체격; 틀, 뼈대

1 "들어오세요."라고 목사가 말했을 때, 그는 악마의 영혼을 보게 될까 두려워했는데, 실제로 그는 그것을 보았다.

"Hello, Reverend," said Chillingworth. "I suspect you will need my medical assistance to help you put your heart and strength into the task of making the election sermon."[2]

"Not this time," answered the reverend solemnly. "My recent walk through the woods has provided me with a renewal of spirit and energy. I will not need any of your drugs."

They both knew that they were no longer trusted friends, but rather bitter enemies.

"Reverend, are you sure you shouldn't use my services to help you make this most important sermon? Heaven knows you may not be here next year to make another one."

"Yes, Heaven grant it, I'll be in a better world," replied the reverend. "But in my present frame of body, I don't need your medicine."

"Well, I'm glad to hear it," said the doctor.

✔ Check Up

Why did the doctor come to see the reverend?

a He wanted to help the reverend write his speech.

b He wanted to bid the reverend farewell.

c He wanted to give the reverend some medicine.   정답: c

---

2 당신이 당선 설교를 쓰는 일에 온 마음과 힘을 쏟을 수 있도록 제 의학적 도움이 필요하지 않을까 생각합니다.

After the doctor left, the reverend called his servant to bring him a large meal. He devoured the food like an animal that had not eaten for a long time. Then he spent all night flinging written pages of his sermon from the desk, as if Heaven was transmitting the words through his hand.[1]

When the reverend awoke in the morning, the pen was still between his fingers, and the sermon was marvelously completed.

On the day of the new governor's inauguration, the marketplace was crowded with the townspeople, who were waiting to see the procession of officials pass and to hear the reverend's sermon.[2] Hester and Pearl joined the crowd.

Everywhere around them were festivities, wrestling matches, and contests. The strict Puritan society was filled with people who were as joyful as they were allowed to be.[3]

□ servant 하인, 하녀
□ meal 식사, 끼니
□ devour 게걸스레 먹다
□ transmit 전달하다
□ marvelously 놀랍게도, 신기하게도
□ inauguration 취임식
□ be crowded with ~으로 붐비다

□ procession 행렬
□ festivity 축제; 경축 행사
□ contest 대회
□ strict 엄격한
□ joyful 기쁜, 반가운, 즐거운
□ festival 축제
□ spot 발견하다 (spot-spotted-spotted)

When Pearl asked if the reverend would be there, Hester said, "Yes, but he won't be joining us. And we shouldn't speak to him if we see him today."

Roger Chillingworth also came to the festival. When Hester first spotted him, he was speaking with the captain of the ship that would be leaving for Europe on the following day.[4]

---

1   그러고 나서 그는 마치 하느님이 자신의 손을 통해 말씀을 전하기라도 하듯, 밤새 책상에 앉아 설교문들을 써댔다.

2   새 주지사의 취임식 날, 시장은 마을 사람들로 가득했다. 그들은 관리들의 행렬이 지나가는 것을 보고 목사의 설교를 듣기 위해 기다리고 있었다.

3   엄격한 청교도 사회는 자신들에게 허락된 만큼 즐거워하는 사람들로 가득했다.

4   헤스터가 처음 그를 발견했을 때, 그는 다음 날 유럽으로 떠나는 그 배의 선장과 얘기를 나누고 있었다.

When Hester later spoke to the captain, he told her
that Chillingworth would be joining them on the
voyage. Her heart sank at the fearful news, and
when she saw Chillingworth, she felt his smile hid a
terrible, secret meaning. But Hester had no time to
think about the captain's shocking news.

The time was at hand for the reverend to give his
sermon. When she saw the Reverend Dimmesdale,
she felt as though he were another person whom she
had never seen before.[1] She felt sad, as if he were in
another world.

Then Hester saw Mistress Hibbins, who asked her
if she had met the reverend in the forest recently.
Hester denied it. But Mistress Hibbins continued to
tell her that the reverend had been there and signed
his name in the Black Man's book. She said the

□ voyage 항해
□ fearful 두려운, 무시무시한
□ shocking 충격적인
□ at hand 가까이에, 가까운 장래에

□ continue to부정사 계속 ~하다
□ deny 부인하다
□ outlying 바깥에 있는, 멀리 떨어진
□ encircle 에워싸다, 둘러싸다

1 딤스데일 목사를 보았을 때, 그녀는 그가 예전에 한 번도 본 적이 없는 다른 사람인 것 같이 느껴졌다. → as though: 마치 ~인 듯 (= as if)

2 악마는 자신의 명부에 서명했음을 인정하지 않으려는 사람들에게 낙인을 남기는 방법을 갖고 있다고 그녀가 말했다. → those who: ~하는 사람들

Black Man had his way of leaving a mark on those who would not admit they had signed his book.[2]

To make matters worse for Hester Prynne, the festival had brought to town many people from outlying areas.[3] These people encircled her, staring and pointing at her mark of shame.

✔ Check Up

What terrible news did the ship's captain tell Hester?

a That the doctor would also be sailing on the ship

b That the ship would be delayed for several months

c That the reverend would not be leaving with them   정답 : b

---

3 헤스터 프린에게는 설상가상으로, 축제가 열리자 멀리 떨어진 지역에서 많은 사람들이 마을로 왔다. → to make matters worse: 설상가상으로

On this day, Hester felt more pain than she had on the first day she had worn the letter. What nobody knew was that the same mark of disgrace burned on the saintly Reverend Dimmesdale.[1]

□ **disgrace** 불명예, 망신, 치욕
□ **saintly** 신앙심이 깊은, 거룩한
□ **eloquent** 웅변의, 감명적인, 설득력 있는
□ **pedestal** 대, 받침대, 연단
□ **profound** 심오한
□ **inspire** 영감을 주다
□ **reach** ~에 도달하다, ~에 닿다
□ **peak** 절정
□ **glory** 영광
□ **meanwhile** 그러는 동안, 한편

1 아무도 몰랐던 사실은 똑같은 불명예의 낙인이 신앙심 깊은 딤스데일 목사의 몸에서도 불타고 있다는 것이었다.

98

It was at this time that the reverend's powerful and eloquent voice could be heard throughout the marketplace, coming from a high pedestal at the eastern end of the marketplace.[2] People were brought to silence by his profound words. Many people said that never before had they heard so wise, so high, and so holy a spirit speak as they heard on that day.[3]

Through his powerful waves of Heaven-inspired words, the reverend reached his proudest peak of glory, as he stood atop the pedestal.

Meanwhile, Hester and Pearl stood next to the old scaffolding with the symbol still burning on her breast.

✔ Check Up

다음 중 본문의 내용을 가장 잘 요약한 것은?

a Hester's most shameful day was also the reverend's greatest.

b Many newcomers made Hester feel ashamed.

c The reverend delivered Heaven's profound words.

정답: a

2 목사의 힘차고 감동적인 목소리가 시장 전체에 들린 것은 이때였으며, 그것은 시장의 동쪽 끝에 있는 높은 연단에서 울려 퍼졌다.

3 많은 사람들이 말하기를, 그날처럼 그렇게 현명하고, 그렇게 고결하고, 그렇게 성스러운 영혼이 말하는것을 들어 본 적이 없다고 했다.
  → 부정어구(never)가 문두에 나오면 주어와 조동사가 도치된다.

When the reverend's sermon was finished, music began, and a procession of honorable town fathers began walking on a pathway through the crowds of people.[1]

When they reached the western end of the marketplace, the people cheered. As the shouts died down, Hester saw the reverend, and was shocked at how very pale and weak he looked. It was as if he had used the last of his energy to deliver his powerful and grand sermon.[2] Now he appeared to be a feeble man who could barely stand by himself. Pastor Wilson hurried to the reverend's side and tried to hold his arm for fear that he would fall, but the reverend shook him off.[3] He kept walking on his own, like a shaky infant. By this time, he was very near the old scaffold.

The crowd looked at him in shock, wondering if his earthly faintness was just another sign of his

□ honorable 고결한; 명예로운	□ shake off ~을 털어내다, 따돌리다
□ pathway 좁은 길, 오솔길	□ on one's own 스스로, 혼자 힘으로
□ cheer 환호하다, 갈채하다	□ shaky 흔들리는, 휘청거리는
□ deliver 전달하다; (연설, 설교 등을) 하다	□ by this time 이때쯤
□ grand 웅장한, 인상적인	□ wonder if... ~인지 아닌지 궁금해 하다
□ appear to 부정사 ~처럼 보이다	□ faintness 연약함, 희미함
□ feeble 연약한, 허약한	□ hold out (팔 등을) 뻗다
□ barely 간신히	□ invisible 보이지 않는

heavenly strength.[4] Suddenly, the reverend turned toward the scaffold and held out his arms.

"Hester," he cried, "my little Pearl, come here to me!" The look on his face was one of terrible pain. But Pearl ran to him and threw her arms around him. Hester, as if forced by invisible hands, slowly approached him.

1 목사의 설교가 끝나자, 음악이 시작되고 명예로운 마을 원로들의 행렬이 사람들을 뚫고 좁은 길을 지나가기 시작했다.

2 그는 마치 강력하고 인상적인 설교를 하기 위해 마지막 힘을 다 소진한 것 같았다.

3 윌슨 목사는 딤스데일 목사가 쓰러질까봐 서둘러 옆으로 가서 그의 팔을 붙잡으려고 했지만, 딤스데일 목사는 그를 뿌리쳤다. → for fear that...: ~할까 두려워, ~하지 않도록

4 군중들은 충격 속에서 그를 바라보며, 그의 속세의 연약함이 그의 신성한 힘의 또 다른 징표가 아닐까 궁금해 했다.

- support 지탱하다; 후원하다, 부양하다
- blacken 검게 하다
- cast 던지다 (cast-cast-cast)
- pit 구덩이; 함정
- dishonor 불명예, 망신
- tempter 유혹자; 악마, 사탄
- in an uproar 몹시 떠들썩하여
- noble 귀족
- rank 고위, 고관; 계급, 등급
- dignity 고위인사, 고관
- guilty 유죄의, 죄가 있는
- act (연극의) 막

Together, with Hester supporting the reverend's weight and Pearl holding his hand, they climbed up the steps of the scaffolding together.

"Are you mad?" whispered Roger Chillingworth, who stood near them. "Stand away from that woman and child! You will blacken your good name and be cast into the pit of dishonor! I can't help you after this!"

"Ha ha," the reverend laughed at Chillingworth. "Tempter, you are too late this time. With God's help, I will escape you now!"

The crowd watched in an uproar as the three stood on the scaffolding. The noble men of rank and dignity could not understand the meaning of his actions.

Old Chillingworth followed them, as if he were just another actor in their guilty drama, on stage for the final act.[1] Looking darkly at the reverend, he said, "You could have searched the Earth for a place to hide from me. There is no place high or low where you could have escaped to, except for this very scaffolding."[2]

---

[1] 늙은 칠링워스는 그들을 따라 마치 자기가 그들의 유죄 드라마에 출연한 또 다른 배우인 것처럼 마지막 막을 위해 무대로 올라갔다.

[2] 높던 낮던 바로 이 처형대 말고는 당신이 도망칠 수 있었던 장소는 없군.

The reverend looked to Hester, "Isn't this better than the plans we made in the forest?"

"I don't know. It may lead to the death of us all," she replied.

"God will protect you and Pearl. As for me, I am a dying man. This is my last chance to accept the truth of my shame."

Then, the reverend faced the other clergymen, the governor, the noblemen, and the crowd of townspeople.

"People of New England!" he cried in a solemn and majestic voice. "Behold me, a shameful sinner! I should have stood here seven years ago when the governor demanded to know the name of Hester Prynne's partner in sin![1] You have all seen the scarlet letter that this woman wears. But there has stood one among you whose brand of shame and infamy

☐ lead to ~에 이르다
☐ as for ~에 관해서
☐ majestic 위엄 있는, 장엄한
☐ brand 낙인
☐ infamy 불명예, 악명

☐ at this point 이때쯤
☐ collapse 쓰러지다; 무너지다
☐ manage to부정사 그럭저럭 ~하다, 간신히 ~하다
☐ step forward 앞으로 나서다
☐ witness 목격하다, 보다; 입증하다

1 7년 전, 주지사가 헤스터 프린과 함께 죄를 지은 상대의 이름을 알고자 요구했을 때 전 이곳에 섰어야 했습니다.

2 하지만 여러분이 보지 못한 치욕과 불명예의 낙인이 찍혀 있는 또 한 사람은 여러분 사이에 있었습니다!

you have not seen!"[2]

At this point, the reverend's weakness was so great that he nearly collapsed. But he managed to stand by himself and stepped forward, away from Hester and Pearl. "But now you must witness the great power of the Lord and the true mark of shame. Behold!"

One Point

At this point, the reverend's weakness was **so great that** he nearly collapsed. 이때쯤 목사의 허약함은 너무 심해서 그는 쓰러질 뻔했다.

so + 형용사 + that절: 아주 ~해서 …하다

ex. She was **so happy that** she couldn't say a word.
그녀는 너무 기뻐서 한 마디도 할 수 없었다.

With a quick motion, the reverend tore away his holy robe to expose his bare chest. The crowd was horror-stricken as they gazed upon the terrible miracle emblazoned upon the flesh of his breast.[1] The reverend had a look of victory on his face shortly before he collapsed to the floor of the scaffold.

Hester raised his head in her hands, and old Chillingworth knelt down by him and said, "You have escaped me! You have escaped me!"

"My little Pearl," the reverend said to the child beside him. "Will you kiss me now?"

The girl leaned forward and kissed his lips. And with her kiss, the spell of grief that had been over her all her life was broken.[2] Her tears fell on her father's cheek.

"Farewell, Hester," said the reverend.

□ motion 움직임, 동작
□ tear away 찢어 버리다 (tear-tore-torn)
□ horror-stricken 공포에 사로잡힌
□ gaze upon ~을 뚫어지게 보다
□ miracle 기적
□ emblazon 문장으로 꾸미다
□ victory 승리
□ kneel down 무릎을 꿇다 (kneel-knelt-knelt)

□ spell 주문
□ grief 슬픔, 비탄; 고난, 고통
□ tear 눈물
□ farewell 안녕
□ praise 칭찬, 찬양
□ breath 숨, 호흡
□ still 움직이지 않는, 정지한
□ awe 외경, 경외심

"Shall we not meet again in Heaven? Shall we not spend our eternal lives together? Certainly we've paid enough of a price for that," she said to him.

"Only merciful God knows," said the reverend. "If He had not brought me here to tell the truth to these people, I would have been lost forever.[3] Praise to His name! His will is done! Farewell!"

With that word came the reverend's last breath. The crowd was silently still, in a state of shock and awe.

✔ *Check Up*

How did the doctor feel about the reverend's actions?

a He felt elated.

b He felt disappointed.

c He felt victorious.

정답 : q

---

1 군중들은 그의 가슴 살에 새겨진 끔찍한 기적의 흔적을 뚫어지게 응시하면서 공포에 사로잡혔다.

2 키스를 하자, 평생 그 아이에게 드리워져 있었던 슬픔의 주문이 풀렸다.

3 만약 그분이 이 사람들에게 진실을 말하도록 나를 이곳으로 인도하지 않았더라면, 나는 영원히 방황했을 것이오. → 가정법 과거완료 문장

As the days passed, many people spoke of the scarlet letter, just like Hester's, that they had seen imprinted on the reverend's breast.[1]

Some thought he had inflicted it upon himself through terrible self-torture. Others thought that Roger Chillingworth had used drugs and magic spells to inflict it upon him.[2] And still others believed that Heaven had placed it there to punish him for his sin.

imprint (도장 등을) 누르다, 찍다
inflict A upon B A를 B에 가하다
magic 마법의
religious 종교적인
authorities <복수형> 당국
defend 변호하다; 방어하다
character 인격, 품성

declare 선언하다
guilt 죄
moment 순간
example 보기, 예; 모범
moral 교훈; 도덕상의
stand out 눈에 띄다, 두드러지다
ultimately 궁극적으로

Many of the religious authorities defended Reverend Dimmesdale's character and pronounced that his dying words declared no guilt in the matter of Hester Prynne and her daughter. They said that the reverend had merely used his last Earthly moments to deliver a powerful sermon through his own example.[3] But the moral that stood out from the poor reverend's miserable experience was ultimately, "Be true! Be true! Be true!"

1 며칠이 지나도록 많은 사람들은 헤스터의 것과 똑같이, 자신들이 보았던 목사의 가슴에 새겨진 주홍글씨에 대해 얘기했다.

2 또 어떤 사람들은 로저 칠링워스가 그것을 그의 몸에 새기기 위해 약과 마법의 주문을 사용했다고 생각했다.

3 그들은 목사가 자기 자신의 예를 통해 강력한 설교를 하려고 지상에서의 마지막 순간을 이용한 것뿐이라고 말했다.

After the object of Roger Chillingworth's quest for revenge was gone, the old man simply withered away into nothing.[1] He died within the same year and left a great amount of money and property to Hester Prynne's little daughter Pearl.

Pearl and Hester disappeared for some time after that. But eventually, Pearl became the richest heiress in the New World, and Hester Prynne returned to her little cottage to continue her simple existence of hard work and charity.[2]

□ object 대상; 목적
□ quest 탐색, 탐구
□ wither away 시들다
□ nothing 하찮은 사람
□ a great amount of 상당한 양의
□ property 재산
□ disappear 사라지다
□ eventually 결국, 마침내
□ heiress 상속녀
□ existence 존재

□ bury 묻다, 매장하다
□ along with ~와 함께
□ share 공유하다
□ blank 공백의
□ tombstone 묘석, 묘비
□ mysteriously 불가사의하게
□ appear 나타나다
□ shield 방패; 방패꼴 문장
□ engrave 새기다, ~에 조각을 하다
□ inscription 비문

1 로저 칠링워스의 복수를 위한 탐색 대상이 사라진 후, 그 노인은 그저 하찮은 사람으로 점점 시들어갔다. → be gone: 없어지다, 사라지다

2 그러나 결국 펄은 신세계에서 가장 부유한 상속녀가 되었고, 헤스터 프린은 그녀의 작은 오두막으로 돌아와 힘든 노동과 자선활동으로 소박한 삶을 계속 이어갔다.

When she finally died at a very old age, she was buried next to an unmarked grave, which along with hers shared a single blank tombstone.[3] Some years later, there mysteriously appeared a shield engraved on the tombstone. If one were to read it, they would see the inscription, "On a Black Background, the Letter A in Red."[4]

✔ *Check Up*

본문의 내용과 일치하면 T, 일치하지 않으면 F를 쓰세요.

ⓐ Hester and Pearl lived out their lives in luxury.   ____
ⓑ After Dimmesdale died, Roger seemed to have nothing to live for. ____

정답: a F b T

3 그녀가 아주 많은 나이로 마침내 세상을 뜨자, 이름 모를 무덤 옆에 묻혔고, 그 무덤과 그녀의 무덤은 아무것도 적히지 않은 하나의 묘비를 공유했다.

4 누군가 그것을 해독할 수 있다면, '검은 바탕에 붉은 A자'라는 비문을 보게 될 것이다.
    → 여기서 be to부정사는 '~할 수 있다'라는 가능을 나타낸다.

Comprehension Quiz

A 보기에서 알맞은 단어를 골라 다음 문장을 완성하세요.

> devoured   frame   occupied   crowd

1. While he was ____________ with the task, there came a knock on the door.

2. But in my present ____________ of body, I don't need your medicine.

3. He ____________ the food as if he were an animal that had not eaten for a long time.

4. Hester and Pearl joined the ____________.

B 다음 중 옳은 설명은 **T**, 틀린 설명은 **F**에 표시하세요.

1. Hester Prynne did not tell Dimmesdale that Chillingworth was her husband.   T   F

2. Pearl was happy when Dimmesdale kissed her.   T   F

3. Reverend Dimmesdale and Hester held hands and kissed in the forest.   T   F

4. Hester told Reverend Dimmesdale that she and Pearl would go away with him.   T   F

Answers

A   1 occupied   2 frame   3 devoured   4 crowd
B   1 F   2 F   3 T   4 T

C 다음 질문에 맞는 답을 고르세요.

❶ What did Hester do after she and Reverend Dimmesdale agreed to run away together?

(a) She gave him a big kiss on the lips.

(b) She slapped his face.

(c) She took the scarlet letter off her breast.

❷ What happened when Pearl kissed Reverend Dimmesdale's lips on the scaffolding?

(a) She was arrested.

(b) The spell of grief over her life was broken.

(c) She had to wear a scarlet A.

D 내용 전개에 맞게 다음 문장을 다시 배열하세요.

❶ Reverend Dimmesdale became angry that Hester hadn't told him Chillingworth was her husband.

❷ Reverend Dimmesdale and Hester Prynne decided to leave the colony.

❸ People encircled Hester Prynne, staring and pointing at the mark on her bosom.

❹ Reverend Dimmesdale wrote his election sermon enthusiastically.

❺ Hester Prynne begged Dimmesdale to forgive her.

_______ ⇨ _______ ⇨ _______ ⇨ _______ ⇨ _______

---

*A*nswers

C ❶ (c) ❷ (b)

D ❶ ⇨ ❺ ⇨ ❷ ⇨ ❹ ⇨ ❸

권말 부록

리스닝 길잡이

리스닝 길잡이

이제는 CD를 가지고 〈주홍글씨〉를 귀로 즐겨 봅시다. 영문을 들을 때에는 아래의 듣기
요령과 함께 영어의 특징적인 발음 현상 몇 가지만 알고 있으면 훨씬 쉽게 알아들을 수 있습니다.

첫째 영어의 리듬을 타세요.

우리말은 각 글자가 모두 한 박자씩이라면 영어는 절대 그렇지 않습니다. 영어는 발음이 강한
부분과 약한 부분이 연속되면서 리듬을 만들어 냅니다. 즉 단어마다 있는 강세가 문장의 강세가
되어 각 문장마다 고유한 리듬을 만들어 나가게 되는 것입니다. 따라서 영어를 말하거나 들을
때 영어의 리듬을 타는 것은 필수적입니다. 이 리듬이 몸에 익으려면 연습이 많이 필요합니다.
우선 우리는 각 단어의 강세가 어디에 있는지 파악하는 것부터 시작합시다.

둘째 강하게 들리는 말 위주로 들으세요.

영어에서는 의미를 전달하는 데 중요한 역할을 하는 단어나 표현을 강하게 발음합니다. 따라서
크게 들리는 말부터 신경 쓰세요. 영어를 처음 들을 때에는 모든 단어를 다 듣는 것보다는 자기
가 듣는 말이 무슨 의미인지 파악하는 것이 우선입니다. 작게 들리는 말은 대부분 관사나 조동
사 등 전체 내용에서 주요한 역할을 하지 못하는 것입니다. 지금 단계에서는 무시하셔도 좋습니
다.

셋째 이어지는 말에 주의하세요.

영어는 눈으로 볼 때에는 단어들이 각각 떨어져 있어 문제 없지만 들을 때는 사정이 달라집니다.
우리말과 마찬가지로 영어도 옆의 단어와 음이 합쳐지는 경우가 많습니다. 예를 들어 '옷을 벗
다'의 의미인 take off는 [테이크 어프]가 아니라 [테이커프]처럼 한 단어처럼 들리게 됩니다.

★ 이제 영어 리스닝에서 주의해야 할 매우 기초적인 사항을 알게 되었습니다.

116

섀도잉하기

이번에는 영어를 들으면서 한 가지 재미있는 연습을 해봅시다.

섀도잉(shadowing)이라는 것입니다. shadow가 '그림자'란 의미이죠? 이 단어가 동사로는 '그림자처럼 따라다니다'의 뜻이 있습니다. 바로 테이프에서 성우가 하는 말을 몇 박자 뒤에 그대로 따라하는 것입니다. 성우가 말하는 속도, 그리고 힘을 주는 부분, 약하게 읽는 부분, 말을 멈추는 부분을 앵무새처럼 똑같이 따라해 보세요.

자기도 모르는 사이에 영어 말하기와 듣기 실력이 쑥쑥 늘어날 것입니다. 이 방법은 전문가들 사이에서도 효과가 입증되어 있답니다. 물론 각각의 어구와 문장들이 무슨 뜻인지 생각하면서 읽으셔야겠죠.

1 단계 자기가 따라할 수 있는 부분까지 듣고 테이프를 멈춘다. 그리고 큰 소리로 따라한다.

2 단계 자기가 따라할 수 있는 부분까지 듣고 큰 소리로 따라한다. 소리 내어 말하는 동시에 테이프에서 나오는 소리를 들으며 돌림노래 부르듯 따라한다.

3 단계 갈수록 좀더 많이(문장 한 개 정도 분량) 듣고 섀도잉한다.

주의! 항상 자신이 어떤 내용을 읽고 있는건지 생각하세요.

CHAPTER ONE   : page 10-11

 #1

    Although the (❶) (   ) the Boston Colony strove to create a utopian society, two of the first things they built when they made their town were a cemetery and a prison. On this day, twenty years after the (❷) (   ) settlers arrived in the New World colony, the townspeople gathered outside the prison.

    "Good women," proclaimed one woman, "If we judged wicked women like Hester Prynne, she (❸) not have the easy sentence that the town magistrates have handed her!"

    "Yes!" agreed (❹) (   ). "They should at least brand the mark upon her forehead with a hot iron! By placing the mark on the front of her gown, she can cover it up anytime!"

    "Yes!" cried another, "She may cover it as she likes, but the mark will always be on her heart!"

    Then the prison door, covered in iron spikes, flew open. A large, (❺) figure in black came out from the inner darkness.

다음은 〈주홍글씨〉의 도입 부분입니다. 처음이 잘 들리면 계속해서 부담이 없지요. 우선 이 앞 부분을 들어 보세요. 그리고 괄호 안이 어떻게 들리는지 귀 기울이십시오. 또한 이어지는 각 발음에 대한 설명을 잘 읽어 보세요. 영어의 대표 발음 현상을 위주로 알기 쉽게 해설했으니 여기에 나오지 않는 부분도 문제없이 들을 수 있을 것입니다.

❶ **forefathers of** [f포어f파더r저비] forefathers의 -s와 of가 이어지면서 한 단어처럼 발음된다. 앞 단어가 자음으로 끝나고 이어지는 단어가 모음으로 시작하면 십중팔구 연음이 된다.

❷ **first Puritan** [f퍼스퓨뤼튼] first의 -st와 Puritan의 P-가 이어지면서 3개 자음이 연속하게 되었다. 이런 경우, 가운데 자음은 흔히 발음하지 않는다. 따라서 just, last처럼 -st로 끝나는 단어들은 뒤에 자음으로 시작하는 단어가 오면 t는 소리나지 않는다.

❸ **would** [웃/우] could, would, should 등의 조동사는 명료하게 발음되는 경우가 없다. 조동사, 전치사, 관사, 대명사 등 문장의 의미에 그다지 중요한 역할을 하지 않는 요소들은 빠르고 약하게 발음된다. 위의 세 단어도 [쿳/쿠], [웃/우], [슛/슈] 정도로 스치듯 소리난다.

❹ **another woman** [어/으나더r 워먼] another는 2음절에 강세가 있어, 상대적으로 1음절은 매우 약해진다. 1음절이 모음으로만 된 경우는 특히 그렇다. 이때 another의 a가 [ə]에서 [ə]로 변하기 십상이다. 강세를 받지 못하는 [i], [e] [ə] 등의 음은 종종 [ə]로 약화된다. 한편 woman은 '우먼'이 아니라 [**워먼**]처럼 발음된다. 우리에게 익숙한 단어나 고유명사 등은 막상 들을 때 우리가 잘 알고 있는 소리로 절대 들리지 않는다. 따라서 접할 때마다 발음과 강세를 익혀두자.

❺ **frightening** [f프**롸**이트닝 / f프**롸**잇으닝] frightening은 발음이 두 가지다. 후자의 경우 -en을 발음하기 전에 잠시 [읏] 하고 숨을 멈추었다가 콧소리를 내며 이어지는 음을 발음하는 것이다. 예를 들어, gotten도 [**가튼**] 또는 [**갓은**]처럼 소리나는데, 이는 [tn], [tl]음에서 주로 일어나는 현상이다.

With his hand, he (**1**   ) (   ) usher out a young woman. But she pushed the hand away and stepped out into the open by her won free will, with an air of dignity.

In the woman's arms was a three-month-old baby. The baby winked because it was the first time it had ever (**2**   ) (   ) on its face. The mother, standing fully revealed amid the townspeople, lowered the baby in her arm to (**3**   ) (   ) (   ). She was blushing, but she wore a proud smile. On the breast of her gown was a large (**4**   ) A. The letter was made of fine, red cloth and embroidered with rich, gold thread. The design was artistic and fanciful.

Hester Prynne was a tall young woman, with an elegant figure and dark gleaming hair. Those who knew her were amazed at her beauty and ladylike comportment under these circumstances.

"She certainly has (**5**   ) (   ) with the sewing needle," remarked one of the women, "but what a shameful way to show it!"

"Make way in the King's name!" shouted the prison officer. "Everyone will have a chance to (**6**   ) (   ) good view of this wicked woman from now until noon. Come along, Hester. Show your scarlet letter in the marketplace!"

❶ **tried to** [트롸이투 / 츄롸이투] tried의 -ed[d]와 to의 t가 이어지면서 한번에 소리 난다. 영어에서는 비슷한 음이 이어지면 한번에 소리나는 경향이 있다. 한편 to는 [튀] 보다는 [테]에 가깝게 소리난다. to가 강세를 받지 않기 때문에 약하게 발음되기 때문 이다.

❷ **felt sunlight** [f펠(ㅌ)썬라잇] felt의 t는 매우 약하게 발음되거나 아예 소리나지 않는다. 또한 sunlight는 '선라이트'가 아니다. 마지막 [t]음이 앞 모음의 받침처럼 발 음돼 '잇' 처럼 해야 자연스럽다.   p, t, k, s, b, d, g 등으로 끝나고 바로 앞에 모음이 있으면, 마지막 음은 앞 모음의 받침처럼 발음한다.

❸ **show her gown** [쇼우허r가운 / 쇼우어r가운] her는 발음이 약해져서 [허], 심지 어는 [어r]로 들리기도 한다. 대명사, 조동사, 전치사, 접속사, 관사 등 의미상 중요한 역할을 하지 않는 단어들은 문장 안에서 약하고 빠르게 발음된다. 영어는 이렇게 강약 이 이어지면서 특유의 리듬이 생기는 것이다. 특히 had, have 등과 같은 h로 시작하 는 조동사와 he, him, her 등 h로 시작하는 대명사는 강세를 받지 못하면서 h음이 종종 탈락된다.

❹ **letter** [레러] 모음 사이에 있는 t 또는 tt는 종종 [r]로 발음된다. 이는 미국영어의 대 표적인 현상이다.

❺ **great skill** [ㄱ뤠잇 ㅅ끼일] great은 '그레이트'가 아니라 [ㄱ뤠잇]처럼 해야 자연 스럽다.   skill은 -k-가 'ㄲ'처럼 소리나는데, 이는 s- 다음에 p, t, k 음이 이어지면 된 소리로 발음되는 경향 때문이다.

❻ **get a** [게뤄 / 게더] 모음 사이에 있는 t 또는 tt가 [r]로 소리나는 이 현상은 한 단어 뿐만 아니라 이렇게 두 단어가 이어지면서 단어들 사이에서도 일어난다.

istening Comprehension

A 등장인물에 대한 설명을 잘 듣고 맞는 기호를 쓰세요.

ⓐ Hester Prynne

ⓑ Roger Chillingworth

ⓒ Dimmesdale

ⓓ Pearl

❶ ______________________________ ______

❷ ______________________________ ______

❸ ______________________________ ______

❹ ______________________________ ______

B 다음을 듣고 문장의 빈칸을 채우세요.

❶ The __________ of Boston Colony strove to create a __________ society.

❷ She was __________ to be in the __________ of the crowd.

❸ When Hester refused, Pearl ________ into a fit of tears and an ear-piercing ________.

❹ She smiled ________ and looked down at the symbol on her ________.

❺ The reverend __________ __________.

*A*nswers

A ❶ A strange child that was suspected of being a demon. – ⓓ
❷ This person had a scarlet letter inscribed on his breast. – ⓒ
❸ This person was forced to stand on a scaffolding with her baby for three hours.– ⓐ
❹ This person sought revenge on Reverend Dimmesdale. – ⓑ

B ❶ forefathers, utopian ❷ relieved, pesence ❸ burst, scream ❹ drearily, bosom
❺ remained, speechless

C 다음 질문을 듣고 받아쓴 다음, 맞는 답을 고르세요.

❶ _________________________________ ?

(a) He was traveling around the world.

(b) He was in medical school.

(c) He was being held prisoner by the heathen savages.

❷ _________________________________ ?

(a) He got it done at a tattoo parlor.

(b) He enscribed it on himself as self-punishment

(c) Hester Prynne carved the A into his chest.

D 다음을 듣고 받아쓴 다음 옳은 설명은 **T**에, 틀린 설명은 **F**에 표시하세요.

❶ _________________________________ T F

❷ _________________________________ T F

❸ _________________________________ T F

❹ _________________________________ T F

❺ _________________________________ T F

---

*A*nswers

C ❶ Where was Roger Chillingworth before he came to Boston Colony? (c) / ❷ What was one explanation for the scarlet A inscribed on Reverend Dimmesdale's chest? (b)

D ❶ When Hester Prynne came out of the prison, she stood with strength and dignity. (T) ❷ Reverend Dimmesdale insisted that they should take Pearl away from her mother. (F) / ❸ Roger Chillingworth was a kind old doctor, who never wanted to hurt anybody. (F) / ❹ Reverend Dimmesdale said he could not remember the time when he and Hester Prynne sinned together. (F) / ❺ Some people thought that God placed the scarlet letter on Reverend Dimmesdale's breast as a punishment for his sin. (T)

전문 번역

p. 10-11 보스턴 식민지의 선조들은 이상적인 사회를 만들어 내기 위해 노력했지만, 그들이 마을을 만들 때 처음 세운 것 중 두 가지가 바로 묘지와 감옥이었다. 최초의 청교도 정착민들이 신세계 식민지에 도착한 후 20년이 흐른 이날, 마을 사람들이 감옥 밖에 모였다.

"선한 여인들이여."라고 한 여인이 크게 말했다. "우리가 헤스터 프린 같은 부도덕한 여인들을 심판한다면, 그녀는 마을 치안판사들이 그녀에게 내린 그런 가벼운 형량을 선고받진 않을 거예요!"

"맞아요!"라고 또 다른 여인이 맞장구쳤다. "그들은 적어도 그녀의 이마에 뜨거운 쇠로 낙인을 찍어야 합니다! 드레스 앞쪽에 낙인을 단다면 그 여자는 언제든 그것을 가릴 수 있어요!"

"맞아요!"라고 또 다른 여인이 외쳤다. "그녀는 자기 좋을 대로 그것을 가릴지도 몰라요. 하지만 그 낙인은 그녀의 가슴 위에 영원히 있을 거예요!"

그때 쇠못으로 뒤덮인 감옥 문이 열렸다. 검은 옷을 입은 우람하고 무시무시한 사람이 어두운 안쪽에서 나타났다. 그는 손으로 젊은 여인을 이끌려고 했다. 그러나 그녀는 그 손을 뿌리치고 위엄 있는 태도로 자진해서 광장으로 걸어 나왔다.

p. 12-13 그 여인의 팔에는 세 달된 아기가 안겨 있었다. 아기는 처음으로 얼굴에 햇볕을 받았기 때문에 눈을 깜빡거렸다. 마을 사람들 한 가운데 완전히 모습을 드러낸 채 서 있는 아기 엄마는 드레스를 보여주기 위해 팔에 안긴 아기를 밑으로 내렸다. 그녀는 얼굴을 붉혔지만 당당한 미소를 짓고 있었다. 드레스의 가슴 부분에는 커다란 A자가 있었다. 그 글자는 고급스런 빨간 천으로 만들어졌으며 값진 금색 실로 수가 놓여 있었다. 그 디자인은 예술적이고 환상적이었다.

헤스터 프린은 키가 큰 젊은 여인으로 우아한 자태에 윤기나는 검은 머리를 하고 있었다. 그녀를 아는 사람들은 이런 상황 속에서도 그녀의 아름다움과 기품 있는 태도에 깜짝 놀랐다.

"바느질 솜씨가 정말 뛰어나군." 여인들 중 한 사람이 말했다. "하지만 그것을 보여주기엔 정말 수치스런 방법이잖아!"

"왕의 이름으로 길을 여시오!"라고 간수가 소리쳤다. "모든 사람들은 지금부터 정오까지 이 부도덕한 여인을 잘 볼 수 있을 거요. 따라와요, 헤스터. 시장에서 당신의 주홍글씨를 보여주시오!"

p. 14-15 구경꾼들 사이에 길이 열렸고, 헤스터 프린은 공개적인 처벌이 약속된 장소로 걸어갔다. 그녀는 차분하게 보스턴에서 가장 오래된 교회 옆에 있는 시장 서쪽 끝의 처형대로 갔다. 처형대는 시민들로 하여금 법에 복종하게 하기 위해 공개적으로 처벌이 행해지는 곳이다. 그곳에는 사람의 머리를 단단히 고정시켜서 대중의 시선을 받도록 만들어진 형틀이 있었다. 그러나 헤스터 프린은 그런 벌을 선고받지 않았다. 그녀의 형벌은 3시간 동안 단 위에 서 있는 것뿐이었다.

그녀는 계단을 올라가 형벌을 받기 시작했다. 구경꾼들은 엄숙한 침묵 속에서 그녀와 주홍글씨를 바라보았다. 헤스터는 사람들의 야유와 모욕을 마주할 각오가 되어 있었다. 그러나 그녀는 그들의 무거운 침묵이 더 참기 힘들다는 것을 알게 되었다. 그곳에 서 있을 때 추억들이 떠오르기 시작하면서 그녀의 마음은 과거로의 여행을 떠나기 시작했다. 그녀는 행복했던 어린 시절을 보고 느낄 수 있었다. 그리고는 거울을 보고 있는 자신의 얼굴과 얼굴에서 풍기는 젊고 아름다운 광채를 보았다. 그런 다음 그녀는 훨씬 나이가 많은 한 남자의 얼굴을 보았다. 은둔해서 오랜 세월 동안 공부를 하는 바람에 그의 눈은 흐릿했고 피부는 창백했다. 그의 몸은 약간 기형이어서 왼쪽 어깨가 오른쪽보다 조금 높았다.

p. 16-17　그때 헤스터 프린의 추억여행은 끝이 났다. 그리고 그녀는 다시 처형대 위에서 마을 사람들에게 둘러싸여 있는 자신을 발견했다. 그들은 여전히 그녀와 그녀의 가슴에 있는 주홍글씨를 뚫어지게 쳐다보았다. 그녀는 가슴 위의 글씨를 내려다보며 그것이 현실이라는 걸 직접 확인하기 위해 그것을 만졌다. 그것은 그녀의 아기와 지독한 수치심이 그렇듯이 실제였다.

　그곳에 잠시 서 있은 후에 헤스터는 군중들 한켠에 있는 사람을 보았다. 그녀는 그를 무시할 수 없었다. 그는 인디언 옆에 서 있는 백인이었다. 주름진 얼굴에 몸집이 작은 그 백인 남자는 문명화된 옷과 야만스러운 옷을 뒤섞어 입고 있었다. 그는 자신의 신체적 특징을 감추려고 애썼지만, 왼쪽 어깨가 오른쪽 어깨보다 높은 게 확실했다. 그를 보면서 그녀는 아기를 너무 꼭 안는 바람에 아기가 아파서 울었지만, 그녀는 듣지 못한 듯 했다.

　이 마을의 이방인인 그 남자는 헤스터 프린을 마주 보았다. 처음에 그의 시선은 무심했지만, 그녀가 처한 상황을 파악하기 시작하자 그의 얼굴엔 공포스런 표정이 떠올랐다.

p. 18-19　"말씀 좀 묻겠습니다, 선생님." 그 남자는 마을 사람에게 말했다. "이 여인은 누구이며 왜 저런 공개적인 치욕을 겪어야 하는 겁니까?"

　"이 마을 분이 아니시군요."라고 그 마을 남자는 말했다. "이곳에 사는 사람이라면 누구나 헤스터 프린과 그녀의 부도덕한 행실에 대해 알고 있지요. 그녀는 딤스데일 목사님의 교회 신도들 사이에서 엄청난 물의를 일으켰어요."

　"맞습니다. 저는 이 마을 사람이 아니오. 저는 오랫동안 남쪽에 있는 미개한 이교도들의 포로였습니다. 제게 이 여인, 헤스터 프린의 죄에 대해 말씀해 주십시오."

　"저 여자는 어느 영국 학자의 아내입니다. 그는 우리 식민지에 합류하기로 결정하고 부인을 먼저 보냈습니다. 하지만 이 남자에게서는 2년 동안 소식이 들리지 않았고, 그의 젊은 아내는 자신의 어리석은 판단을 따랐던 거죠."

　"아, 무슨 말씀인지 알겠어요."라고 낯선 남자는 쓴웃음을 지으며 말했다. "그렇다면 지금 그녀가 안고 있는 아기의 아버지는 누구인가요?"

　"바로 그것이 모든 사람들이 궁금해 하는 의문입니다." 하고 마을 남자가 말했다. "프린 부인은 또 다른 죄인의 이름을 말하길 거부하고 있습니다."

　"그녀의 남편이 와서 그 수수께끼를 풀어야겠군요."라고 그 낯선 사람이 말했다.

p. 20-21　"네, 그가 아직 살아 있다면 그래야 하죠." 하고 그 마을 남자가 맞장구쳤다. "이런 범죄의 형벌은 보통 사형입니다. 하지만 치안판사들이 자비를 베풀었습니다. 왜냐하면 그

126

녀의 남편이 아마도 바닷속에 가라앉아 있을 것이기 때문이지요. 하지만 앞으로 그녀는 남은 평생 동안 간음한 자임을 나타내는 주홍색 표식을 달고 있게 될 겁니다.”

“현명한 처벌이군요.”라고 그 이방인은 말했다. “그녀의 표식은 죄에 대한 살아 있는 설교 역할을 할 겁니다. 그녀의 상대였던 죄인이 그녀 옆에 서 있지 않다는 사실에 화가 나는군요. 그를 찾아서 알려야 해요. 그래야 해요!”

그 낯선 사람이 가버릴 때 헤스터 프린은 그에게서 눈을 떼지 않았다. 그녀는 군중들 앞에 있다는 사실에 안도했다. 그 남자를 혼자 마주 대하지 않아도 되기 때문이었다.

갑자기 그녀는 어떤 목소리 때문에 자신의 생각에서 깨어났다. “헤스터 프린, 당신은 지금 내 말을 들어야 합니다!” 치안판사들이 판결을 선언할 때 사용되는 근처 교회의 발코니에 벨링햄 주지사가 서 있었다. 그 발코니에는 주지사 및 그의 수행원들과 함께 다른 귀족들도 서 있었다.

헤스터 프린은 발코니를 향했다. 그녀가 들은 건 보스턴에서 가장 나이 많은 존 윌슨 목사의 목소리였다.

p. 22-23 “헤스터 프린.” 늙은 목사는 말을 이었다. “나는 여기 있는 당신의 담임 목사인 딤스데일 목사에게 말했소. 당신을 이런 슬픈 타락의 길로 유혹한 부도덕한 남자의 이름을 지금 당장 말하게 해야 한다고 말이오.”

그러자 벨링햄 주지사가 말했다. “딤스데일 목사, 그녀의 담임 목사로서 당신은 그녀의 영혼에 대한 책임이 있소. 그녀가 말을 하도록 촉구해서 그녀의 회개를 증명해야 하오.”

그것에 답하기 위해 딤스데일 목사는 군중에게 연설을 하려고 자리에서 일어났다. 그 목사는 유명한 영국의 대학 중 한 곳을 졸업한 젊은 사제였다. 힘 있는 목소리와 인상 깊은 지성 덕분에 그는 이미 자신이 봉사하는 식민지 주민들에게서 엄청난 존경과 찬양을 받고 있었다.

“형제님, 이 여인에게 얘기하시오.”라고 윌슨 목사는 재촉했다. “당신은 그녀의 영혼을 구원할 수 있는 유일한 사람이오!”

딤스데일 목사는 처형대 위에 서 있는 여인을 보았다. “헤스터 프린.” 그가 말을 시작했다. “당신은 훌륭한 윌슨 목사님의 말씀을 들었소. 당신과 함께 죄를 저지른 사람의 이름을 말하도록 권유하는 바이오. 그러면 두 사람 모두 마음의 평화를 얻을 것이오. 그에 대한 잘못된 동정심이나 약한 마음 때문에 침묵을 지켜서는 안 됩니다.”

헤스터 프린의 품에 안긴 아기도 목사의 힘찬 목소리를 느꼈다. 아기는 반쯤 행복하고 반쯤 슬픈 표정으로 그를 올려다보았다. 그러나 이런 간청에도 헤스터는 머리를 가로저을 뿐이었다.

p. 24-25 “여인이여, 하늘의 자비심의 한계를 시험하지 마시오!”라고 윌슨 목사는 화난 목소리로 말했다. “이름을 말하시오. 그러면 당신의 회개로 가슴에서 주홍글씨를 족히 뗄 수 있을 거요!”

“절대 말할 수 없어요!”라고 헤스터 프린은 소리쳤다. 그녀는 딤스데일 목사의 눈을 뚫어지게 보았다. “이 글자는 제 가슴에 너무 깊이 박혀서 쉽게 지워질 수 없어요. 제 고통뿐만 아니라 그의 고통도 견뎌내고 싶어요!”

“어서 말해!”라고 처형대 주위에 있던 마을 사람들이 외쳤다. “아기 아버지의 이름을 말해!”

사람들의 가혹하고 차가운 목소리 중 하나를 알아차린 듯 했을 때 그녀의 얼굴이 창백해졌다. 그러나 그녀는 고집했다. “말하지 않을 거예요. 내 아이에게는 속세의 아버지가 절대로 없을 겁니다. 이 아이는 천국의 아버지만 알아야 할 거예요!"

"그녀는 그의 이름을 고백하지 않을 겁니다."라고 딤스데일 목사는 자신의 가슴에 한 손을 얹고 발코니 너머로 몸을 기울이며 속삭였다. "그녀는 말하지 않을 겁죠!"라고 그는 사람들을 향해 말했다.

p. 26-27　헤스터가 감옥으로 돌아왔을 때 그녀는 초조한 히스테리 상태였다. 그리고 아기는 미친 듯이 울어댔다. 간수장 브라켓은 그녀가 자신이나 아기를 해치지 못하도록 계속 그녀를 감시했다. 결국 그는 그녀를 진찰하도록 의사를 데려왔다. 의사는 그녀가 처형대 위에 서 있을 때 그녀에게 관심을 보였던 바로 그 이방인이었다. 그의 이름은 로저 칠링워스였다.

간수가 그를 감방으로 데리고 와 헤스터 프린이 그를 보자, 그녀는 죽은 듯이 꼼짝하지 않았다.

"걱정 마시오."라고 의사가 간수에게 말했다. "제가 프린 부인과 아기를 잘 돌보겠소. 곧 당신의 감옥에 평화와 고요가 깃들 겁니다."

의사는 인디언들에게 배운 지방 고유의 식물에서 추출한 약초 치료제를 만들었다.

"여기 있소, 프린 부인, 이것을 아기에게 먹이세요. 아기는 당신이 직접 줘야 먹을 거예요. 그러면 이게 아기를 진정시킬 겁니다."

헤스터는 그의 손을 밀쳤다. "이 죄 없는 아기를 독살해서 복수하려고요?"라고 그녀가 속삭였다.

"여인이여, 바보처럼 굴지 마시오."라고 그 의사는 차갑지만 달래는 목소리로 대답했다. "나는 이 불쌍한 사생아를 해치지 않을 거요."

그녀는 주저하며 아기에게 그 물약을 주었고, 아기는 곧 편안하게 잠들었다.

p. 28-29　그런 다음 의사는 헤스터 자신을 위한 약을 주었다. 조심스럽게 컵 안을 들여다보며 그녀가 말했다. "당신이 복수를 위해 독약으로 나를 죽이지 않을 거라는 걸 내가 어떻게 알죠?"

"헤스터." 의사가 대답했다. "날 그렇게 몰라서 내 목표가 그렇게 얄팍할 거라고 생각하는 거요? 가슴에 이 강렬한 치욕을 달고 살게 하는 게 무엇보다도 최고의 복수가 아니겠소?"

이 말에 그녀는 살짝 미소를 지으며 약을 먹었다. 약효가 나타나는 동안 의사는 계속 얘기했다. "이런 일이 일어날 거라는 걸 알았어야 했는데. 그랬다면 우리가 결혼한 날 걸어갔던 교회 통로 끝에 저 주홍글씨가 이글거리고 있는 걸 볼 수 있었을 텐데."

"제가 당신에게 늘 정직했다는 걸 당신도 알 거예요." "저는 항상 당신에게 사랑을 느끼지 못한다고 말했어요. 그리고 사랑하는 척 하지도 않았고요. 하지만 미안해요. 제가 당신한테 몹쓸 짓을 했어요."라고 그녀는 그에게 말했다.

"아니오."라고 그가 대답했다. "우린 서로에게 잘못했소. 나는 당신의 꽃피는 젊음이 나의 노쇠함과 이렇게 부자연스럽게 뒤엉키지 말도록 해야 했소. 우리 사이의 저울은 이제 균형이 맞소. 하지만 나는 당신 혼자 이런 치욕을 겪도록 내버려 둔 그 겁쟁이에게 복수할 거요. 당신은 내게 그의 이름을 말하지 않겠지만 내가 찾아내겠소. 꼭 찾아낼 거요. 이제 내가 당신에게 부탁하는 건 당신의 남편이라는 내 정체를 이 마을에서 비밀로 해달라는 것뿐이오. 그리고 내가 복수하려는 그 남자에게 나에 대해 얘기하지 마시오."

"그의 이름을 비밀로 간직한 것처럼 당신의 비밀도 지키겠어요."라고 헤스터가 말했다.

p. 32-33   헤스터 프린의 수감생활은 그 의사와의 상담 직후 끝났다. 그러나 마을 사람들 틈에서의 고통스러운 삶은 이제 막 시작되었다.

그녀는 마음대로 마을을 떠날 수 있었다. 그러나 헤스터는 그곳에 머물며 일생 동안 형벌을 받기로 결심했다. 그녀와 아기는 마을 외곽의 작은 오두막으로 이사했다. 그녀는 노련한 바느질 솜씨로 남부럽지 않게 생계를 꾸려갈 수 있었다. 그러나 그녀는 자신을 위해서는 수입을 거의 쓰지 않았다. 그녀는 어린 딸에게 아주 좋은 옷을 입히고 나머지 돈은 자선 단체에 기부했다.

그녀의 뛰어난 솜씨 때문에 마을 사람들은 항상 그녀에게 일을 맡겼다. 그러나 그들은 얼굴 표정과 말로 그녀에게 수치심을 잊지 못하게 했다.

헤스터의 딸 펄은 진주의 뛰어난 아름다움이나 가치 때문이 아니라 그 위대한 희생 때문에 붙여진 이름이다. 그럼에도 불구하고 아기는 곧 아름답지만 묘한 아이로 자라났다. 딸을 지켜보며 그 아이의 이상한 행동을 알아챘을 때 헤스터는 아이도 주홍글씨와 연관되어 있고 그 영향을 받고 있는 건 아닌지 걱정했다.

p. 34-35   펄이 나이가 들면서 억지로 규칙에 순응시킬 수 없다는 것이 분명해졌다. 아이는 엄마의 아주 간단한 명령도 듣지 않으려 했다. 그리고 아이의 성격은 변덕이 심했다. 헤스터의 영혼이 겪고 있는 전쟁이 펄의 내면에서 벌어지고 있는 것 같았다.

헤스터는 펄이 다른 아이들과 노는 것을 지켜보길 좋아했을 것이다. 그러나 펄은 엄마만큼이나 따돌림을 당했다. 그리고 그녀는 아주 어렸을 때부터 자신의 위치를 받아들였다. 운명은 펄 주변에 깰 수 없는 벽을 만들었다. 펄은 자기 주변에 모여든 마을의 심술궂은 청교도 아이들을 맞닥뜨리면, 작은 야만인처럼 아이들에게 돌을 던지고 소리를 지르며 못되게 변했다.

호전적인 딸을 보자 헤스터는 무릎을 꿇고 물었다. "하느님 아버지, 제가 세상에 낳은 이 아이는 어떤 존재입니까?" 그러면 어린 펄은 엄마가 이렇게 절규하는 소리를 듣고는 엄마를 보며 요정처럼 영리하게 미소를 지을 뿐이었다.

펄에게서 가장 이상한 점 중 하나는, 아기였을 때 그 아이가 처음 관심을 보인 것은 대부분의 아기들과 달리 엄마의 미소가 아니었다는 것이다. 오히려 엄마의 가슴에 달린 주홍색 A자에 먼저 이끌렸다.

p. 36-37   몇 년 후 펄은 사방으로 뛰어다녔다. 어느 날 그 아이는 야생화를 한 아름 꺾었다. 그리고는 엄마의 가슴 위에 있는 글자를 향해 그것들을 던지며 그 중 하나가 주홍글씨에 맞으면 기뻐서 깡충깡충 춤을 추었다.

헤스터가 본능적으로 처음 취한 행동은 두 팔로 글자를 가리는 것이었다. 그러나 그녀는 자기 가슴에 꽃이 고통스럽게 부딪히는 것을 속죄의 일부라 여기며 참아냈다. 엄마가 확연히 고통스러워하는 것을 보고 펄은 눈을 사악하게 번득이며 웃을 뿐이었다.

"너 정말 내 아이 맞니?"라고 헤스터는 농담처럼 물었다. "누가 너를 만들었고 누가 너를 이곳에 보냈지?"

"엄마가 말해 보세요."라고 아주 심각해진 펄이 말했다. "제게 말해 보세요."

"하늘에 계신 아버지가 너를 보냈단다."라고 헤스터는 잠시 말을 멈췄다가 대답했다. 하지만 영리한 아이는 엄마가 망설이는 것을 놓치지 않았다. "하느님은 저를 보내지 않았어요. 저에겐 하늘에 계신 아버지가 없어요!"라고 펄이 소리쳤다.

"아, 제발 이렇게 말하면 안 돼. 하느님은 우리 모두를 창조하셨단다!"라고 헤스터가 외쳤다.

"아니에요. 제게 말해 주셔야 해요."라고 말하면서 펄은 춤추고 돌아다니며 웃었다. "제게 말해 주세요!"

아이의 질문에 대답할 수 없었던 헤스터는 온몸을 떨었다.

p. 38-39 어느 날 헤스터는 펄을 데리고 벨링햄 주지사의 저택으로 갔다. 그녀는 주지사가 수를 놓아 달라고 부탁한 장갑을 돌려 주러 가는 거라고 펄에게 말했다. 그러나 진짜 이유는 마을 사람들이 딸을 그녀에게서 빼앗아 갈 계획이라는 소문을 들었기 때문이다. 그들은 펄이 악령이 씌운 아이일지도 모른다고 의심했다. 그래서 그 아이를 떼어 놓음으로써 헤스터의 영혼을 구원할 계획이었다. 헤스터는 또한 벨링햄 주지사가 이 계획의 주동자라는 얘기도 들었다. 그래서 그와 얘기를 나누기로 마음 먹었다.

그날 그녀는 펄에게 주홍색 A자와 똑같이 금실로 수놓아진 밝은 빨간 색 드레스를 입혔다. 그래서 아이는 주홍글씨가 생명을 지녀 커진 것처럼 보였다.

호화로운 저택에 도착했을 때, 펄은 활짝 핀 장미덤불을 보고는 엄마에게 빨간 꽃 한 송이를 꺾어 달라고 요구했다.

p. 40-41 헤스터가 안 된다고 하자 펄은 울음을 터뜨리며 귀가 찢어질 듯 소리를 질렀다. 하지만 그때 사람들이 자기들에게 다가오고 있는 것을 보자 갑자기 조용해졌다. 그 무리 중에는 벨링햄 주지사, 윌슨 목사, 젊은 아서 딤스데일 목사, 그리고 로저 칠링워스 의사가 있었다. 최근에 딤스데일 목사는 건강이 악화되고 있어서 그를 치료하던 의사는 그의 가깝고도 충실한 동반자가 되었다.

근사한 주홍색 옷을 입은 어린 소녀를 놀란 눈으로 쳐다보던 주지사는 이렇게 물었다. "여기 이 어린 아이는 누구요?"

"아, 이 아이는 불행한 헤스터 프린의 딸입니다."라고 윌슨 목사가 말했다. "이 아이가 최근에 우리들이 얘기했던 바로 그 아이입니다."

"그렇군요."라고 벨링햄 주지사는 말했다. "지금 이 자리에서 이 문제를 논의해 보죠. 헤스터 프린." 그녀 가슴 위의 글자를 똑바로 쳐다보며 그가 말했다. "우리는 당신과 아이의 영혼을 보호하는 것이 우리의 의무가 아닌지에 대해 많은 논의를 했소. 이 아이를 데려가 수수하게 옷을 입히고 하늘과 땅의 진리 속에서 교육을 받게 하는 것이 최선이라고 생각하지 않소?"

"다른 누구보다 제가 딸아이를 잘 가르칠 수 있습니다."라고 헤스터 프린은 손가락으로 글자를 가리키며 말했다. "이걸 통해 배웠으니까요."

"여인이여." 주지사가 말했다. "그것은 치욕의 상징이오. 그리고 우리가 그 아이를 보다 올바른 사람의 손에 맡기는 것이 최선이라고 생각하는 이유요."

p. 42-43 "그렇지만 이 글자는 제게 딸을 보다 현명하고 나은 사람으로 키울 수 있도록 교훈을 가르쳐 주었습니다."라고 헤스터 프린은 차분하게 말했다.

"그것은 우리가 판단할 것이오."라고 벨링햄은 말했다. 그런 다음 그는 의자에 앉아서 펄을 자신의 두 무릎 사이에 두려고 했지만, 엄마 이외에 어느 누구의 손길에도 익숙하지 않았던 아이는 달아났다.

아이들을 잘 다루기로 유명한 윌슨 목사는 계속해서 유심히 살펴보았다. "펄, 누가 너를 만들었는지 내게 말해 줄 수 있니?"

헤스터 프린는 집에서 인간 영혼의 창조에 대한 청교도적인 믿음을 아이에게 교육시켰다. 그러나 펄은 그 진지한 질문에 장난스럽게 대답하기로 마음 먹었다. 그래서 자신은 하늘에서 만들어진 것이 아니라 감옥 문 옆에서 자라고 있는 야생 장미 덤불에서 뽑혔다고 말했다.

"이건 끔찍하군요."라고 주지사는 소리쳤다 "여기 누가 자신을 만들었는지 모르는 세 살짜리 아이가 있어요!"

헤스터는 펄을 팔에 꼭 안았다. "신이 제게서 빼앗아 가신 모든 것에 대한 보상으로 이 아이를 주셨습니다. 이 아이는 저의 행복이자 고통입니다! 여러분이 이 아이를 제게서 빼앗아가기 전에 저는 죽고 말 거예요!"

"펄은 당신이 이 아이에게 해줄 수 있는 것보다 더 나은 보살핌을 받게 될 거예요."라고 나이 많은 윌슨 목사가 말했다.

p. 44-45 "신이 저더러 이 아이를 지키라고 보내신 거예요!"라고 헤스터 프린은 소리쳤다. 그런 다음 그녀는 젊은 딤스데일 목사를 향해 울부짖었다. "제 대신 말씀 좀 해주세요! 당신은 제 담임 목사였으니 제 영혼에 대해 책임이 있으셨어요. 당신은 이분들보다 저를 더 잘 알고 있어요. 저들이 제 아이를 데려가지 못하게 해주세요!"

"그녀의 말은 진실입니다."라고 딤스데일 목사는 강하고 떨리는 목소리로 말했다. "신이 그녀에게 정숙하지 못한 삶을 바꾸도록 가르치기 위해 이 아이를 보낸 겁니다. 두 사람의 관계는 신성합니다. 우리가 뭐라고 신이 그녀에게 아이를 선물하는 실수를 저질렀다고 말합니까? 우리가 뭐라고 그녀의 삶에서 선한 신의 축복을 빼앗아갑니까?"

"말 잘했소."라고 윌슨 목사가 말했다. "벨링햄 주지사님, 어떻게 생각하십니까? 이 선한 목사가 헤스터 프린을 대신해서 설득력 있게 변호를 했습니다."

"정말 그렇군요." 주지사가 대답했다. 펄은 자기 어머니와 함께 있을 것이고, 우린 이 문제에 대해 더 이상 소란을 피우지 않을 것이오. 적절한 시기에 교회 관계자들이 그 아이가 학교와 교회에 가도록 조치를 취하겠소. 이상이오."

그러자 어린 펄은 딤스데일 목사의 손을 잡고 그 손을 자신의 뺨에 대었다. 목사는 주위를 둘러본 다음 그 아이의 이마에 입을 맞췄다.

p. 46-47 "이상한 아이군요."라고 칠링워스 의사가 말했다. "우리가 그 아이의 천성을 자세히 살핀다면 그 아이의 죄 많은 아버지의 정체를 알아낼 수 있을 겁니다."

"그렇게 하는 것은 죄가 될 거요."라고 윌슨 목사가 말했다. "그 문제에 대해선 기도하며 신의 뜻에 맡기는 것이 더 나을 겁니다."

문제가 해결되자 헤스터 프린과 펄은 주지사의 저택을 떠났다. 집 밖에서 그들은 벨링햄 주지사의 사악한 여동생 히빈스 부인을 만났다. 그녀는 몇 년 후 마법을 부렸다는 이유로 처형되었다.

"쉿, 쉿." 그녀가 쉿 소리를 냈다. "오늘밤 악마와 집회를 여는데 우리와 함께 숲으로 가겠소?"

"우린 가지 않을 거예요!"라고 헤스터 프린은 대답했다. "전 딸과 집에 있을 거예요. 하지만 사람들이 제게서 딸아이를 빼앗아 갔다면 당신을 따라가서 제 피로 사악한 악마의 명부에 제 이름을 썼을 거예요!"

이것을 보면 아이가 그렇게 빠른 시기에 악마의 덫에서 헤스터 프린의 영혼을 구했다고 말할 수 있을 것이다.

[제 3 장] 복수

p. 50-51 젊은 딤스데일 목사의 건강이 악화되기 시작한 것은 로저 칠링워스가 의사로서 마을에 정착했을 무렵이었다. 마을 사람들은 아픈 목사와 의사의 등장이라는 우연의 일치를 두고 신의 섭리로 이루어진 기적이라고 생각했다. 그래서 마을의 장로들은 딤스데일 목사의 건강이 칠링워스 의사의 손에 맡겨진 것을 신의 뜻이라고 생각했다.

두 사람은 곧 돈독한 친구가 되었다. 의사가 목사의 병의 원인을 찾으며 시간을 보내는 동안 딤스데일 목사는 칠링워스의 의사로서 그리고 연장자로서의 풍부한 경험에 매료되었다. 칠링워스는 그의 육체적인 병이 괴로운 마음과 생각 때문에 생긴 거라고 확신했다. 그러나 무엇이 목사의 마음을 괴롭히고 있는지 알 수 없었.

두 사람은 곧 같은 집으로 이사했다. 그러나 시간이 지나자 마을 사람들은 칠링워스 의사를 다르게 보기 시작했다. 마을로 이사 온 후 그의 외모와 태도가 눈에 띄게 바뀌었기 때문이다. 한때 그는 차분하고 친절했지만, 이제 마을 사람들은 그의 얼굴에서 악의를 보았다. 목사의 악화된 건강은 악마 때문이며, 악마는 로저 칠링워스의 모습을 빌어 목사 앞에 나타난 것이라는 소문이 마을에 퍼졌다.

p. 52-53 어느 날 목사는 칠링워스가 채집한 식물로 약을 만들곤 하는 실험실로 의사를 찾아갔다. 의사는 자기 집 옆에 있는 묘지에서 채집한 한 다발의 흉측하게 생긴 식물들을 살펴보고 있었다.

"바로 저기 묘지에서 이 잎들을 발견했소."라고 의사는 창밖을 가리키며 말했다. "이런 변종은 처음 봐요. 이것들이 이름 없는 무덤에서 자라고 있는 걸 발견했소. 난 이것이 죽은 남자의 심장에서 자라지 않았나 생각하오. 아마도 이 잎들은 그와 함께 땅에 묻힌 무서운 비밀을 나타내고 있을 거예요. 살아 있는 동안 그것을 고백하는 게 나았을 텐데."

"그는 그러고 싶었지만 그럴 수 없었을 거예요."라고 말하며 목사는 통증 때문에 쑤시는 듯이 가슴을 부여잡았다. "제 교회 신도들은 죄를 고백할 때 항상 큰 안도감을 느낍니다."

바로 그때 의사와 목사는 헤스터 프린과 펄이 묘지를 가로질러 오솔길을 걸어가는 것을 보았다. 펄은 불경스럽게 이리저리 무덤 위를 뛰어다녔다. 그런 다음 우엉 식물에서 가시가 무성한 우엉을 한 줌 뽑아 엄마의 주홍색 A자 라인을 따라 찔러 넣었다.

p. 54-55 "아, 저 아이는 법이나 권위에 대한 존경심이 없군요."라고 로저 칠링워스가 말했다. "요전 날 저 아이가 주지사에게 말 구유통의 물을 뿌리는 걸 보았어요. 도대체 저 아이는

뭐가 잘못된 걸까요?"

갑자기 펄이 창 쪽으로 뛰어오더니 가시가 무성한 우엉 하나를 딤스데일 목사를 향해 던졌다. 그러더니 웃으며 어머니를 불렀다. "엄마, 가요, 그렇지 않으면 악마가 이미 목사님을 붙잡은 것처럼 엄마도 붙잡을 거예요. 빨리 가요. 그렇지 않으면 그가 엄마를 잡아갈 거예요! 하지만 나는 잡지 못하죠!"

"헤스터 프린이 가슴에 저 글자를 달고 치욕을 견디는 것이 마음속에 그것을 숨기고 사는 것보다 덜 비참하다고 생각하세요?" 엄마와 딸이 창가에서 멀어질 때 의사가 목사에게 물었다.

"네, 그렇게 생각해요."라고 목사는 대답했다. "하지만 제가 지금 정말 얘기하고 싶은 것은 바로 제 건강이에요. 고질적인 제 병의 원인에 대한 당신의 소견은 뭔가요?"

"솔직히 말해서, 제게 말하지 못한 어떤 비밀이 있는지 알고 싶어요. 당신의 문제에 대해 제게 모든 것을 털어놓았나요?"라고 의사가 말했다.

p. 56-57 캐내려는 듯한 질문에 목사는 눈에 보이게 당황했다. "하지만… 물론 다 말씀 드렸어요."라고 그는 더듬거렸다. "당연히 지상의 의사에게 결코 털어놓을 수 없는 제 영혼의 일부가 있는 거죠."

"하지만 마음과 영혼을 열어 보이지 않는다면 제가 어떻게 당신의 육신을 치료할 수 있겠습니까?"

이 말에 목사는 갑자기 불같이 화를 내며 의사의 손을 자신에게서 밀어냈다. 이렇게 미친 듯한 행동을 보이며 그는 방을 뛰쳐나갔다.

두세 시간 후에 목사는 의사의 실험실로 돌아와서 갑자기 화를 내서 미안하다며 사과했다. 두 사람은 힘들이지 않고 다시 우정을 이어갔다. 그러나 그날 늦게 목사가 의자에 앉아 잠이 들었을 때 의사가 소리 없이 목사의 방으로 숨어들었다. 의사는 잠자는 목사의 가슴에 손을 얹어 목사의 셔츠를 뒤로 제치고는 그의 맨가슴을 보았다. 의사는 자신이 본 것에 한순간 몸서리를 쳤다. 다음 순간 그의 얼굴엔 행복과 만족감에 들뜬 악마의 표정이 퍼져갔다.

이날 이후 로저 칠링워스와 아서 딤스데일 목사의 관계는 미묘하게 바뀌었다. 의사는 차분한 모습을 유지했다. 그러나 그는 비밀스럽게 목사를 통제하면서 그에 대한 복수를 계획하고 있었다.

p. 58-59 딤스데일은 종종 자신이 저지른 죄에 대해 남몰래 스스로를 벌주었다. 그는 음식도 잠도 없이 지내도록 스스로를 몰아붙이기도 하고, 피투성이가 되도록 스스로를 매질하기도 했다. 그러던 어느 날 밤, 그는 자신을 벌줄 수 있는 새로운 방법을 생각해냈다. 한밤중에 그는 옷을 입고 조용히 집을 나섰다.

마치 꿈속을 걷는 것처럼 목사는 시장의 서쪽 끝, 헤스터 프린이 7년 전에 서 있던 처형대로 갔다.

캄캄한 5월 밤, 목사는 처형대의 계단을 올라가 그 위 연단에 섰다. 그는 마을 전체가 잠들었기 때문에 누구도 자신을 발견할 위험이 없다고 생각했다.

그러나 그곳에 서 있는 동안 그의 마음은 공포감에 압도되었고 가슴속에서부터 불타고 있는 주홍글씨를 느꼈다. 그것이 그의 고통과 병의 원인이었다. 그러다 갑자기 아주 길게 큰 소리로 비명을 지르는 바람에 그는 마을 전체가 잠에서 깨어나 그의 수치스러운 모습을 보러 달려올 거라고 생각했다.

그러나 잠에 취한 마을 사람들은 그의 목소리를 그저 야생동물의 울음소리나 마녀들이 깔깔 거리는 소리라고 생각했음에 틀림없다. 왜냐하면 아무도 달려오지 않았기 때문이다.

p. 60-61 그때 목사는 멀리서 다가오는 불빛을 보았다. 등불 을 든 사람이 누구인지 알아볼 수 있을 정도로 불빛이 가까워졌 을 때, 목사는 그 사람이 윌슨 목사라는 걸 알았다. 목사는 딤스 데일을 알아채지 못하고 지나쳐서 계속 걸어갔다. 딤스데일은 윌슨 목사가 방금 전 세상을 떠났을 윈스로프 주지사의 임종의 방에서 늦게까지 자리를 지키다 돌아가는 것임을 알았다.

월슨 목사가 지나간 후 또 다른 불빛이 다가왔다. 이번에 딤스데일 목사는 그것이 헤스터 프 린과 펄이라는 걸 알 수 있었다.

"헤스터 프린, 당신이오?"라고 목사가 물었다.

"딤스데일 목사님." 헤스터는 어둠 속에서 처형대 위에 서 있는 그를 발견하고는 깜짝 놀라 서 외쳤다. "네, 저와 펄이에요. 우리는 윈스로프 주지사님의 임종의 방에서 오는 길이에요. 그 곳에서 그분의 수의를 만들기 위해 치수를 쟀어요. 지금 오두막으로 돌아가는 중이에요."

"헤스터, 펄, 이리 올라와요."라고 목사가 말했다. "두 사람은 전에 이곳에 올라왔던 적이 있지만 나는 당신과 함께 있지 못했소."

헤스터는 조용히 펄의 손을 잡고 연단의 계단을 올라갔다. 어둠 속에서 목사는 펄의 손을 찾 아 꼭 쥐었다. 신선한 생명의 힘이 그의 심장으로 밀려 들어왔고 혈관으로 피가 빠르게 흘렀다. 무거운 짐이 그의 영혼에서 들어 올려졌다!

p. 62-63 "목사님. 내일 정오에 저와 엄마와 함께 이곳에 서 계실래요?" 어린 펄이 말했다.

"내일은 안 된단다, 하지만 언젠가 그렇게 하마."라고 목사가 대답했다.

"하지만 언제요?" 펄이 물었다.

"심판의 날 하나님 앞에서 너와 네 엄마와 함께 서 있으마."라고 그는 대답했다.

펄은 이 말을 비웃었다. 그리고 갑자기 유성이 반짝이더니 밤하늘을 환하게 밝혔다. 그 광채 속에 주홍색 A자를 가슴에 단 헤스터, 자신의 가슴에 손을 얹은 목사, 그리고 두 사람의 손을 잡은 펄이 서 있었다.

목사가 다시 눈길을 지상으로 돌렸을 때 멀리서 다가오는 사람을 가리키고 있는 펄이 보였 다. 그 사람이 가까이 오자 그들은 로저 칠링워스라는 걸 알았다.

"헤스터, 저 남자는 누구요?"라고 목사가 물었다. "난 저 남자가 무서워졌소. 그를 증오하기 시작했소!"

"그가 누구인지 제가 알려드릴게요."라고 펄이 말했다. 그러더 니 아이는 자신의 입술을 목사의 귀에 대고 말도 안 되는 얘기를 속삭이고는 큰 소리로 웃었다.

"애야, 나를 놀리는 거니?"라고 목사가 물었다.

"목사님은 거짓말쟁이예요." 하고 어린 소녀가 말했다. "목사님 은 내일 정오에 저와 엄마와 함께 여기 서 있지 않을 거잖아요."

134

p. 64-65 "안녕하세요." 처형대로 다가온 로저 칠링워스가 말했다. "이 밤 시간에 여기서 무얼 하고 있소? 잠결에 걸어 다닌 게요?"

"내가 여기에 있는지 어떻게 알았소?" 목사가 두려워하며 물었다.

"당신이 여기에 있는지 몰랐소. 주지사님의 임종의 방에 갔다가 집으로 걸어가고 있었을 뿐이오. 지금 나와 함께 집으로 가는 게 좋을 것 같군요. 그렇지 않으면 내일 설교할 힘이 없을 거요."

"그렇군요. 당신과 집으로 가죠."라고 목사가 말했다. 목사는 돌연 꿈에서 깨어난 것처럼 갑작스레 한기와 우울함을 느꼈다.

처형대 위에서의 밤 이후 헤스터 프린은 목사가 정신을 놓을까봐 걱정되었다. 그녀는 몇 년 전 로저 칠링워스에게 자기 남편이라는 진짜 정체를 숨겨 주기로 약속한 것을 기억했다.

그러나 이제 그녀는 목사에게 칠링워스의 끔찍한 의도에 대해 경고하지 않은 것이 자신의 잘못이라고 느꼈다. 그녀는 칠링워스에게 더 이상 그 약속을 지킬 수 없다고 말하기로 결심했다. 그녀는 목사에게 그를 괴롭히는 사람이 누구인지 알려 주어야 했다.

헤스터는 의사와 얘기하기 위해 오래 기다릴 필요가 없었다. 며칠 후 어느 오후, 그녀는 숲에서 식물을 채집하고 있는 그를 보았다.

"가서 놀아라."라고 그녀는 펄에게 말했다. "나는 의사선생님과 얘기를 나누고 싶구나." 그런 다음 그녀는 칠링워스를 향해 이렇게 말했다. "선생님, 당신과 중요한 문제에 대해 얘기를 나눠야겠어요."

p. 66-67 "아, 헤스터 부인." 그가 미소를 지으며 말했다. "마을 위원회에서 곧 당신의 가슴에서 그 주홍글씨를 떼도록 허락할 거라고 하더군요."

"제가 그걸 끝낼 만한 가치가 있는 사람이라면 저절로 떨어질 거예요."라고 그녀는 대답했다. 그녀는 지난 7년의 세월이 칠링워스를 악마를 닮은 괴물로 탈바꿈시켰다는 걸 깨달았다. 그녀는 복수를 추구하는 삶이 그의 몸과 마음과 영혼을 그렇게 어두운 모습으로 변하게 만들었다는 걸 알았다.

"내 얼굴에 당신이 그렇게 심각하게 볼 만한 뭔가가 있소?"라고 의사가 물었다.

"울고 싶은 기분이 들게 하는 그런 거요."라고 그녀가 대답했다. "하지만 또 한 명의 비참한 남자에 대해 얘기하도록 해요. 7년 전에 저는 당신의 정체를 비밀로 하겠다고 약속했어요. 하지만 제게는 당신이 서서히 죽이고 있는 그 남자를 도울 의무가 있어요. 저는 그에게 당신이 누구인지 얘기해야 해요. 그래야 그가 왜 당신이 자기를 괴롭히는지 이해할 테니까요."

p. 68-69 "그 비겁한 사제는 내 영향력과 저주를 알고 있어요."라고 칠링워스는 말했다. "그는 스스로 그것을 인정하길 너무나 두려워할 뿐이오. 그 세월 동안 당신을 아이와 함께 이 마을에 내맡긴 그런 저급하고 비열한 사람을 돕고 싶어 하다니 어리석구려."

"전 그를 도와야 해요."라고 헤스터가 소리쳤다. "이 주홍글씨가 내게 그렇게 하도록 가르치고 있어요. 나는 당신의 비밀을 더 이상 지키지 않을 거예요."

"가서 그에게 말해요."라고 칠링워스가 말했다. "당신의 착한 마음을 그런 나약한 남자에게 낭비하다니 당신이 불쌍할 뿐이오."

"당신도 불쌍해요."라고 헤스터가 대답했다. "현명한 사람을 악마로 바꿔 버린 그런 증오심으로 고통받다니 정말 가엾어요!"

헤스터는 펄이 강가 아래에서 놀고 있는 걸 발견했다. 어린 소녀는 자신의 드레스 가슴 위에 엄마의 것과 똑같이 녹색 A자를 배열했다.

"아, 펄. 하지만 너의 녹색 A자는 내가 달고 있어야 하는 것과 같은 뜻이 아니란다. 내가 왜 이 글자를 달고 있는지 아니?"

"네, 알아요."라고 펄이 대답했다. "목사님이 자신의 가슴에 손을 얹고 있는 것과 같은 이유 때문이에요."

[제 4 장] 숲

p. 72-73   헤스터는 목사에게 로저 칠링워스의 정체를 밝히려는 결심을 단단히 했다. 헤스터는 목사가 숲속을 지나갈 거라는 걸 알고 있는 어느 날, 그와 우연히 만나기 위해 어린 펄을 데리고 집을 나섰다. 그들이 숲으로 들어섰을 때 펄이 소리쳤다. "엄마, 햇살이 엄마를 사랑하지 않나 봐요! 엄마 가슴 위의 A자 때문에 햇볕이 달아나 숨어버려요!"

"그러면 네가 뛰어가서 잡아 오는 게 좋겠구나!"라고 엄마가 대답했다. 어린 소녀는 실제로 밝은 햇살 속에 서서 해를 붙잡았다.

그들이 숲속 깊이 들어갔을 때 펄은 엄마에게 앉아서 잠깐 쉬자고 말했다.

"얘기 좀 해주세요."라고 펄이 졸랐다.

"무슨 얘기?"라고 헤스터가 물었다.

"철로 된 걸쇠가 달린 커다랗고 무거운 검은 명부를 들고 숲에 나타나는 악마에 대한 얘기요. 그리고 그가 어떻게 사람들에게 자신들의 피로 명부에 이름을 쓰게 하는지 말해 주세요. 엄마는 악마를 만난 적 있어요?"

p. 74-75   "누가 그런 얘기를 하든?" 헤스터 물었다.

"어젯밤에 엄마가 지키고 있던 그 집에 있을 때 할머니가 제가 잠든 줄 알고 그 얘기를 했어요. 그 분은 주홍글씨가 악마가 엄마에게 남긴 흔적이라고 말했어요."

"앞으로 더 이상 묻지 않는다면 네게 악마에 대한 얘기를 해 주마."라고 헤스터가 말했다. "악마를 한번 만난 적이 있는데, 이 주홍글씨는 그의 낙인이란다."

갑자기 헤스터는 숲을 걸어오는 발자국 소리를 들었다.

"펄, 이제 가서 놀아라. 나는 우리 쪽으로 걸어오는 사람과 얘기를 나누고 싶구나."

"그 사람이 악마인가요?"라고 펄이 물었다.

"물론 아니란다, 바보 같긴. 그 사람은 목사님이란다."

"그렇군요."라고 펄이 말했다. 이제 아이는 목사가 어두운 숲을 가로질러 오는 것을 볼 수 있었다. "목사님은 가슴에 손을 얹고 있어요. 그건 목사님이 명부에 자신의 이름을 썼고, 악마가 목사님의 가슴에 낙인을 찍었기 때문이에요. 그런데 왜 목사님은 엄마처럼 바깥쪽에 그걸 달고 있지 않죠?"

"이제 가거라, 아가야!" 헤스터가 소리쳤다. "개울 가까이 있거라. 너무 멀리 가지 말고!"

펄은 혼자 노래를 부르며 멀어져 갔다. 헤스터는 목사가 오솔길을 내려오는 걸 보았다. 그는 전보다 더 약하고 우울해 보였다.

p. 76-77 "아서 딤스데일!" 그녀는 그를 불렀다 "딤스데일 목사님!"

"누구요?"라고 목사는 긴장하며 대답했다. "헤스터, 당신이요?"

"네, 저예요."라고 그녀가 대답했다. 그들은 자신들의 상황 때문에 7년 이상을 단둘이 있지 못했다. 그들 둘 다 서로를 바라보는 것이 불안하면서도 행복했다.

그녀에게서 눈을 떼지 않으며 그가 물었다. "헤스터, 당신은 평화를 찾았소?"

그녀는 쓸쓸하게 미소지으며 자기 가슴 위의 상징을 내려다보았다. "당신은 찾았나요?"

"아니, 어두움과 절망 밖에는 아무것도 찾지 못했소. 나는 신도들에게 청렴을 설교하지만 내 존재의 공허함과 고뇌를 알고 있소. 사탄이 항상 나를 비웃는 것처럼 느껴진다오."

"그렇게 자신을 고문하는 건 옳지 않아요." 헤스터가 말했다. "당신은 오랫동안 깊이 참회했어요. 당신은 자신의 죄를 과거 속에 묻어 두는 법을 배워야 해요."

"아니오, 헤스터."라고 목사는 외쳤다. "나는 나를 감싸고 있는 이런 성스러운 옷을 입을 가치가 없소. 가슴에 A자를 달고 있는 당신은 운이 좋은 거요. 나의 낙인은 내 안에서 타고 있소. 내 죄의 진상을 털어놓을 수 있는 친구가 한 사람만이라도 있다면!"

p. 78-79 "제가 그 친구예요. 그리고 함께 죄를 지은 동반자고요."라고 헤스터는 말했다. 그런 다음 그녀는 오늘 두 사람이 만나는 용건을 목사에게 말하려고 애썼다. "당신에게도 큰 적이 있어요. 그 사람은 당신과 같은 지붕 아래 살고 있어요."

"적이 내 지붕 아래서 살고 있다고?" 목사는 놀라며 말했다. "무슨 뜻이오?"

"아, 아서."라고 헤스터가 외쳤다. "저를 용서해 주세요. 오래 전에 저는 당신을 속이겠다고 약속했어요. 사람들이 로저 칠링워스라고 부르는 그 늙은 의사는 제 남편이었어요!"

끔찍하게 사나운 표정이 목사의 얼굴에 퍼져갔다. 그는 땅에 주저앉으며 두 손에 얼굴을 묻었다.

"그걸 알았어야 했는데!"라고 목사는 신음했다. "그를 만난 첫날부터 내 마음은 그가 끔찍한 비밀을 숨기고 있다고 얘기하고 있었소. 왜 내가 알지 못했을까? 아, 헤스터 프린! 이건 당신 책임이오. 나는 당신을 절대 용서할 수 없소!"라고 그는 소리쳤다.

헤스터 프린은 목사에게 팔을 두르고는 그를 가까이 끌어안았다. 그의 뺨이 주홍글씨에 닿았다. 그는 벗어나려고 했지만 그녀는 그를 놓아주려 하지 않았다.

"당신은 나를 용서해야 해요."라고 그녀는 같은 말을 반복했다. "당신은 용서해야 해요."

p. 80-81 "용서하겠소."라고 목사가 부드럽게 말했다. "이제 당신을 용서하겠소. 우린 세상에서 가장 못된 죄인들이 아니오. 그 늙은이의 복수는 나의 죄보다 더 사악하오. 그는 냉혹하게 나를 죽이고 있소. 우리가 저지른 죄는 그 정도로 나쁘진 않소."

"맞아요. 우리가 한 일에는 나름대로 신성함이 있었어요. 우리가 사랑을 나눌 때 서로에게 그렇게 말했잖아요."라고 그녀가 속삭였다. "잊었나요?"

"아니오, 잊지 않았소."라고 그가 속삭였다.

그날은 그들 인생에서 가장 우울한 날이었다. 하지만 그 어두움 속에는 함께 머물고 싶게 만드는 그런 마력이 있었다. 그들은 손을 맞잡고 키스를 하면서 어두운 숲에 앉아 있었다.

"로저 칠링워스는 당신이 자기 정체를 밝힐 거라는 걸 알고 있소."라고 목사는 말했다. "이제 그는 마을 사람들 앞에서 나를 손가락질할 것이오.

"아뇨, 그는 사람들에게 당신의 죄를 발설하지 않을 거예요. 그는 복수를 위한 자신의 음흉한 열정을 만족시킬 만한 비밀스러운 다른 방법들을 찾아낼 거예요. 당신은 그 끔직한 사람에게서 달아나야 해요!"라고 그녀가 말했다.

"맞아요. 그는 나를 죽일 거요."라고 목사는 흥분해서 말했다. "하지만 내가 무얼 할 수 있겠소, 헤스터? 도와주시오, 제발!"

 "바다가 당신을 이 신세계로 데려왔으니 이제 당신을 다시 유럽으로 데려갈 수 있을 거예요. 당신은 영국으로 돌아가야 해요. 아니면 독일이나 프랑스, 혹은 이탈리아에서도 살 수 있을 거예요."

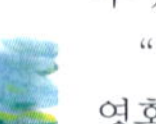

"하지만 어떻게 이곳에서의 내 직을 버릴 수 있겠소? 내 영혼이 망가진다 해도 나는 다른 사람들을 도와야 하오."

"당신이 고통의 무게에 짓눌려 망가진다면 누구도 도울 수 없어요. 이곳을 떠나야 해요."라고 그녀가 말했다. "미래는 새로운 성공의 기회들로 가득 차 있을 수도 있어요. 그냥 앉아서 죽는 것 말고 다른 일을 하세요!"

"아, 헤스터. 나는 이곳에서 죽어야 하오. 낯설고 추운 세계로 혼자 돌아갈 만한 힘이나 용기가 내게는 없소."

그러자 헤스터는 아주 낮은 목소리로 대답했다. "당신은 혼자 가지 않을 거예요."

이 말을 듣고 아서 딤스데일은 기쁨과 희망에 들떠 그녀의 눈을 들여다보았다.

"우리 뒤돌아보지 말아요. 과거는 지나갔어요. 보세요!"

그런 다음 그녀는 손가락으로 가슴에서 주홍글씨를 떼어내더니 그것을 개울가에 있는 바위 위로 세차게 던져 버렸다. 주홍글씨는 그곳에 떨어져 잃어버린 보석처럼 반짝거렸다.

 치욕과 고통의 짐이 가슴에서 사라지자 헤스터는 안도의 한숨을 푹 내쉬었다. 지금 느끼는 자유는 그 글자의 무게가 실제로 어떠했는지를 깨닫게 해주었다. 헤스터는 모자를 벗고 검고 아름다운 머리가 어깨로 흘러내리게 내버려 두었다. 그러자 햇살이 나무 꼭대기를 뚫고 내려와 숲으로 밀려들었다.

헤스터는 기쁨이 가득한 눈으로 다시 목사를 바라보며 말했다. "이제 당신은 우리의 어린 펄을 알아야 해요. 당신은 그 아이를 보았지만 실제로 아직 그 아이를 잘 몰라요. 그 아이는 묘한 아이예요. 하지만 당신은 그 아이를 진심으로 사랑하게 될 거예요."

"그 아이가 나를 알고 싶어 할 거라고 생각하오?"라고 목사가 희망에 차서 물었다. "나는 항상 어린 펄이 두려웠소."

"아, 그건 정말 슬프군요."라고 헤스터는 대답했다. "그 아이는 당신을 진심으로 사랑할 거예요. 그 아이는 지금 멀지 않은 곳에 있어요. 제가 아이를 부를게요. 펄! 펄!"

펄은 멀리서 엄마를 위해 꽃들을 모으고 있었다. 그 아이는 엄마가 부르는 소리를 듣고 천천히 그들이 있는 곳으로 되돌아갔다.

"이리 오너라."라고 헤스터가 말했다. "네가 목사님의 진정한 친구가 되었으면 좋겠구나."

하지만 펄은 엄마의 말을 따르지 않았다. 그 아이는 주홍글씨가 사라진 엄마의 가슴을 가리키며 발을 구를 뿐이었다.

p. 86-87 "알겠어요." 하고 헤스터가 말했다. "어린 아이들은 자신이 늘 알고 있던 것들이 조금이라도 바뀌는 걸 보고 싶어 하지 않아요. 저 아이는 태어난 날부터 보아왔던 글자가 그리운 거예요." 헤스터는 개울가에 있는 글자를 가리키며 말했다. "글자가 저기 있단다, 펄. 이제 그걸 내게 가져오너라."

"엄마가 직접 가져오세요."라고 펄이 말했다.

아이 때문에 낙담한 헤스터는 한숨을 쉬며 개울가로 걸어가서 그 글자를 다시 가슴에 달았다.

"이제 엄마를 알겠니, 아가야?"라고 그녀가 딸에게 물었다.

"네, 이제 엄마는 진짜 내 엄마예요!"라고 말하며 어린 펄은 개울을 가로질러 뛰어서 그들에게 왔다.

"이리 와서 목사님을 만나 보거라, 펄. 목사님이 너와 인사하고 싶으시대. 이분은 너를 사랑하신단다. 너도 이분을 사랑할 거지?"라고 헤스터가 물었다.

"목사님이 정말 우리를 사랑해요?" 펄은 날카롭고 영리한 눈으로 엄마를 보며 물었다. "이분이 우리와 손을 잡고 마을로 걸어갈 건가요?"

"지금은 아니란다, 아가야."라고 헤스터가 말했다. "하지만 곧 우리와 늘 함께 계실 거란다."

"그리고 늘 가슴에 손을 얹고 계실 건가요?"라고 펄이 물었다.

아이의 질문들에 당황한 딤스데일은 자신에 대한 아이의 생각이 누그러지길 바라며 아이에게 몸을 굽히고는 이마에 입을 맞췄다.

하지만 그의 입술이 이마를 떠나자마자 아이는 개울로 달려가 마치 더러운 것이라도 묻은 양 이마에서 키스 자국을 씻어냈다. 그런 다음 엄마와 목사가 가까운 미래에 함께 할 계획을 의논하는 동안 두 사람에게서 멀리 떨어져 있었다.

[제 5 장] 폭로

p. 90-91 숲을 떠난 후 목사는 두 사람의 만남이 실제로 있었다는 걸 믿을 수가 없었다. 그들은 유럽의 도시가 새로운 삶을 시작하기에 최상의 장소라는 결론을 내렸다. 그리고 우연히도 보스턴 항구에 나흘 후 구세계로 떠날 예정인 배가 들어와 있었다. 자선활동을 통해 헤스터는 그 배의 선장을 알게 되었고 자신과 목사와 펄이 그 배로 떠나도록 준비할 수 있었다.

헤스터가 목사에게 준비상황을 얘기하자 그는 뛸 듯이 기뻐하며 이렇게 말했다. "내가 사흘 후에 당선 설교를 하게 되어서 얼마나 다행인지 모르오."

새로운 주지사의 취임을 축하하는 당선 설교는 뉴잉글랜드 성직자의 경력에 절정이 되는 것이었다.

딤스데일은 헤스터와 얘기를 나눈 후 아주 이상하리 만큼 육체적으로 엄청난 힘을 느끼며 집으로 돌아왔다. 그는 자신이 무슨 일을 하더라도 지칠 수 없다고 생각했다.

p. 92-93 마침내 목사는 가장 중요한 당선 설교문을 쓸 수 있는 고요하고 고독한 서재로 들

어갔다. 그가 그 일에 몰두하고 있을 때 문을 두드리는 소리
가 들렸다. 목사는 "들어오세요."라고 말하면서 악마의 영혼
을 보게 될까봐 두려워했는데, 실제로 그는 그것을 보았다.
노크를 한 사람은 로저 칠링워스였다. 목사는 말이 없었다.

"안녕하시오, 목사님." 칠링워스가 말했다. "목사님이 당
선 설교문을 만드시는 데 온 마음과 힘을 쏟을 수 있도록 제
의학적 도움이 필요하지 않을까 생각했습니다."

"지금은 아닙니다."라고 목사는 차분하게 말했다. "최근 숲을 산책하고 났더니 제 영혼과 원
기가 새로워졌습니다. 그러니 당신의 약은 필요 없을 거요."

두 사람은 서로가 더 이상 믿을 만한 친구가 아니라 철천지 원수라는 것을 알고 있었다.

"목사님, 이렇게 중요한 설교문을 쓰는 데 제 도움이 필요없다는 게 확실한가요? 내년에 또
다른 설교문을 쓸 때 당신이 이곳에 없을지도 모른다는 것은 하느님만이 아실 겁니다."

"그래요. 제발 내가 더 나은 세계에 있기를 바라오." 하고 목사가 대답했다. "하지만 지금
내 몸 상태로는 당신의 약이 필요 없습니다."

"그 말을 들으니 기쁘군요."라고 의사는 말했다.

p. 94-95   의사가 방을 나간 후 목사는 하인을 불러 푸짐한 식사를 가져오게 했다. 그는 오
랫동안 먹지 못한 짐승처럼 게걸스럽게 음식을 먹었다. 그리고는 마치 하느님이 자신의 손을
통해 말씀을 전하기라도 하듯이 밤새 책상에 앉아 설교문들을 써댔다.

목사가 아침에 잠에서 깨었을 때 펜은 아직 그의 손가락 사이에 있었으며 놀랍게도 설교문
은 완성되어 있었다.

새로운 주지사의 취임식 날 시장은 마을 사람들로 가득했
다. 그들은 관리들의 행렬이 지나가는 것을 보고 목사의 설
교를 듣기 위해 기다리고 있었다. 헤스터와 펄도 사람들 속
에 있었다.

그들 주변에선 온통 축제와 레슬링 경기와 대회들이 열리
고 있었다. 엄격한 청교도 사회는 자신들에게 허락된 만큼
즐기는 사람들로 가득했다.

펄이 목사도 그곳에 올 거냐고 묻자 헤스터는 말했다. "그래, 하지만 그분은 우리와 함께 있
지 않을 거야. 그러니 오늘 그분을 보더라도 말을 걸어서는 안 돼."

로저 칠링워스도 축제에 왔다. 헤스터가 처음 그를 발견했을 때 그는 다음 날 유럽으로 떠나
는 배의 선장과 얘기를 나누고 있었다.

p. 96-97   나중에 헤스터가 선장과 얘기를 나눌 때 그는 칠링워스도 여행에 그들과 동행할
것이라고 말했다. 그 무시무시한 소식에 그녀의 심장은 철렁 내려앉았다. 그리고 칠링워스를
보자 그의 미소가 끔찍하고 비밀스러운 의미를 감추고 있다고 느껴졌다. 그러나 헤스터는 선장
의 충격적인 소식에 대해 생각할 시간이 없었다.

목사가 설교할 시간이 가까워진 것이다. 딤스데일 목사를 보았을 때 그녀는 그가 예전에 한
번도 본 적이 없는 다른 사람인 것 같이 느껴졌다. 마치 그가 다른 세상에 있는 것처럼 슬프게
느껴졌던 것이다.

그리고 헤스터는 히빈스 부인을 보았다. 그녀는 헤스터에게 최근에 숲속에서 목사를 만났는

지 물어 보았다. 헤스터는 아니라고 대답했다. 그러나 히빈스는 계속 그녀에게 목사가 그곳에 있었고 악마의 명부에 이름을 썼다고 말했다. 그녀는 악마가 자신의 명부에 서명했음을 인정하지 않으려는 사람들에게 낙인을 남기는 방법을 갖고 있다고 말했다.

설상가상으로 축제가 열리자 외부 지역 사람들이 마을로 많이 왔다. 그들은 헤스터의 치욕의 낙인을 보면서 손가락질을 하며 그녀를 둘러쌌다.

p. 98-99　이날 헤스터는 그 글자를 처음 달았던 날보다 더 큰 고통을 느꼈다. 아무도 몰랐던 사실은 똑같은 불명예의 낙인이 신앙심 깊은 딤스데일 목사의 몸에서도 불타고 있다는 것이었다.

목사의 힘차고 설득력 있는 목소리가 시장 전체에 들린 것은 이때였으며, 그것은 시장의 동쪽 끝에 있는 높은 연단에서 울려 퍼졌다. 사람들은 그의 심오한 말에 입을 다물었다. 많은 사람들이 말하기를, 그날처럼 그렇게 현명하고, 고결하고, 성스러운 영혼이 말하는 것을 들어 본 적이 없다고 했다.

연단 위에 서 있을 때 목사는 하느님의 영감을 얻어 파도처럼 힘차게 밀려드는 말을 통해 가장 자랑스러운 영광의 절정에 도달했다.

한편 여전히 가슴에 불타는 상징을 달고 있던 헤스터와 펄은 낡은 처형대 옆에 서 있었다.

p. 100-101　목사의 연설이 끝나자 음악이 시작되고 명예로운 마을 원로들의 행렬이 사람들 사이를 뚫고 좁은 길을 지나가기 시작했다.

그들이 시장 서쪽 끝에 다다랐을 때 사람들은 환호성을 질렀다. 환호성이 잠잠해지자 헤스터는 목사를 보았고 그가 얼마나 창백하고 약해 보이는지 깜짝 놀랐다. 마치 그는 강력하고 인상적인 설교를 하기 위해 마지막 남은 모든 힘을 다 소진한 것 같았다. 이제 그는 겨우 혼자 서 있을 수 있을 정도로 허약해 보였다. 윌슨 목사는 그가 쓰러질까봐 서둘러 딤스데일 목사 옆으로 가서 그의 팔을 붙잡으려 했지만 딤스데일은 그를 뿌리쳤다. 그는 비틀거리는 아기처럼 계속 혼자 걸어갔다. 그때쯤 그는 낡은 처형대에 아주 가까이 있었다.

군중들은 충격 속에서 그를 바라보며, 그의 속세의 연약함이 그의 신성한 힘의 또다른 징표가 아닐까 궁금해 했다. 갑자기 목사가 처형대쪽을 바라보며 양팔을 벌렸다.

"헤스터." 그가 외쳤다. "내 딸 펄, 이리 와요!" 그의 얼굴은 끔찍하게 고통스러운 표정을 지었다. 그러나 펄은 그에게 달려가 두 팔로 그를 껴안았다. 헤스터는 마치 보이지 않는 손에 밀려가듯 천천히 그에게 다가갔다.

p. 102-103　목사의 체중을 지탱해 주는 헤스터와 그의 손을 잡은 펄과 함께 그들은 처형대 계단을 올라갔다.

"미쳤어요?"라고 그들 가까이 서 있던 로저 칠링워스가 속삭였다. "그 여자와 아이에게서 떨어져요! 당신은 자신의 훌륭한 이름을 더럽히고 불명예의 구덩이 속으로 내던져질 거요! 그 후에는 나도 당신을 도울 수 없어요!"

"하하" 목사가 칠링워스를 비웃었다. "이 악마야, 이번엔 너무 늦었다. 하느님의 도움으로 이제 나는 너에게서 도망칠 것이다!"

세 사람이 처형대 위에 섰을 때 군중들은 소란하게 지켜보고 있었다. 지위가 높은 귀족들은 그의 행동의 의미를 이해할 수 없었다.

늙은 칠링워스는 그들을 따라 마치 자기가 그들의 유죄 드라마에 출연한 또 다른 배우인 것처럼 마지막 막을 위해 무대로 올라갔다. 그는 어두운 얼굴로 목사를 보며 이렇게 말했다. “당신은 지구상에서 내게서 숨을 장소를 찾을 수 있었을 텐데. 높던 낮던 처형대 말고는 당신이 도망칠 수 있었던 장소는 없군. “

p.104-105 목사는 헤스터를 보았다. “이것이 우리가 숲에서 세운 계획보다 낫지 않소?”

“잘 모르겠어요. 이 일 때문에 우리 모두 죽을지도 몰라요.”라고 그녀가 대답했다.

“신이 당신과 펄을 보호해 줄 거요. 나로 말하면, 난 죽어가는 사람이오. 이것이 내 죄의 진실을 인정할 마지막 기회요.”

그런 다음, 목사는 다른 사제들과 주지사와 귀족들과 마을 사람들을 향해 섰다.

“뉴잉글랜드 주민 여러분!” 그는 엄숙하고 장엄한 목소리로 외쳤다. “부끄러운 죄인인 저를 보십시오. 저는 7년 전 주지사가 헤스터 프린과 함께 죄를 지은 상대의 이름을 알아내려고 했던 그날 이곳에 섰어야 했습니다. 여러분 모두 이 여인이 달고 있는 주홍글씨를 보았습니다. 하지만 또 한 사람은 여러분 틈에 있었습니다. 여러분은 그에게 찍혀 있는 치욕과 파렴치의 낙인을 보지 못했습니다!”

이때, 목사는 너무 힘이 빠져서 쓰러질 뻔했다. 그러나 그는 가까스로 혼자 서서 헤스터와 펄로부터 한 발짝 앞으로 걸어 나갔다. “하지만 이제 여러분은 신의 위대한 힘과 진정한 치욕의 낙인을 보아야 합니다. 보십시오!”

p. 106-107 빠른 동작으로 목사는 자신의 성의를 찢고 맨가슴을 드러냈다. 군중들은 그의 가슴살에 새겨진 끔찍한 기적의 흔적을 뚫어지게 응시하면서 공포에 사로잡혔다. 목사의 얼굴엔 승리의 표정이 번졌다. 그리고 잠시 후에 그는 처형대 바닥에 쓰러졌다.

헤스터는 손으로 그의 머리를 들었고, 늙은 칠링워스는 그의 옆에 무릎을 꿇고 말했다. “당신은 내게서 벗어났소! 당신은 내게서 벗어났소!”

“내 딸 펄아, 이제 내게 키스해 주겠니?”라고 목사는 자기 옆에 있는 아이에게 말했다. 아이는 앞으로 몸을 숙여 그의 입술에 키스했다. 그 키스와 함께 평생 그 아이에게 드리워져 있었던 깊은 슬픔의 주문이 풀렸다. 아이의 눈물이 아버지의 뺨에 떨어졌다.

“안녕, 헤스터.”라고 목사가 말했다.

“하늘에서 다시 만나지 못할까요? 우리의 영원한 삶을 함께 보내지 못할까요? 우리는 그에 대한 대가를 분명 충분히 치렀어요.”라고 그녀는 그에게 말했다.

“그건 자비로운 신만이 아실 거요.”라고 목사는 말했다. “그 분이 이 사람들에게 진실을 말하도록 나를 이곳으로 인도하지 않았다면 나는 영원히 방황했을 거요. 신의 이름을 찬양하시오. 신의 뜻이 이루어졌소! 안녕!”

그 말과 함께 목사는 마지막 숨을 내쉬었다. 사람들은 충격과 경외감에 사로잡혀 숨을 죽이고 꼼짝하지 않았다.

p. 108-109 며칠이 지나도록 많은 사람들은 헤스터의 것과 똑같이, 자신들이 보았던 목사의

142

가슴에 새겨진 주홍글씨에 대해 얘기했다.

　어떤 사람들은 그가 끔찍한 자기 고문을 통해 그것을 자기 몸에 새겼다고 생각했다. 또 어떤 사람들은 로저 칠링워스가 그것을 그의 몸에 새기기 위해 약과 마법의 주문을 사용했다고 생각했다. 그리고 어떤 사람들은 여전히 하느님이 그의 죄를 벌하기 위해 그것을 거기에 새겨 놓았다고 믿었다.

　많은 종교 권력자들이 딤스데일 목사의 인격을 변호했고 그가 죽어가며 한 말은 헤스터 프린과 그녀의 딸 문제에 무죄를 선언한 것이라고 발표했다. 그들은 목사가 자신의 예를 통해 강력한 설교를 하기 위해 지상에서의 마지막 순간을 이용한 것뿐이라고 말했다.

　하지만 가엾은 목사의 불행한 경험에서 두드러진 확실한 교훈은 결국 "진실하라! 진실하라! 진실하라!"는 것이었다.

p.110-111　로저 칠링워스는 복수의 대상이 사라지자 하찮은 존재로 점점 시들어갔다. 그는 같은 해에 세상을 떠났고 헤스터 프린의 딸 펄에게 많은 돈과 재산을 남겼다.

　그 후 한동안 펄과 헤스터는 마을에서 사라졌다. 그러나 결국 펄은 신세계에서 가장 부유한 상속녀가 되었고, 헤스터 프린은 작은 오두막으로 돌아와 힘든 노동과 자선활동을 통해 소박한 삶을 계속 이어갔다.

　마침내 아주 많은 나이에 세상을 뜨자 그녀는 이름 모를 무덤 옆에 묻혔고, 그 무덤과 그녀의 무덤은 아무것도 적히지 않은 묘비 하나를 공유했다. 몇 년이 흐른 후 신비하게도 묘비에 방패 모양의 문장이 새겨져 나타났다. 누군가 그것을 해독할 수 있다면 "검은 바탕에 붉은 A자"라는 비문을 보게 될 것이다.

〈행복한 명작 읽기〉 집필진

Scott Fisher
Seoul National University (M.A. - Korean Studies)
Michigan State University (Asian Studies)
Ewha Womans University, Graduate School of Translation and Interpretation, English Professor

David Hwang
Michigan State University (MA - TESOL)
Ewha Womans University, English Chief Instructor, CEO at EDITUS

Louise Benette
Macquarie University (MA - TESOL)
Sookmyung Women's University, English Instructor

Brian J. Stuart
University of Utah (Mass Communication / Journalism)
Sookmyung Women's University, English Instructor

David Desmond O'Flaherty
University of Carleton (Honors English Literature and Language)
Kwah-Chun Foreign Language High School, English Conversation Teacher

Michael Souza
University of California, Davis (B.A. Anthropology)
California State University, Dominguez Hills (M.A. Humanities)
Elementary school teacher, Sacramento, California Freelance Writer

Silayan Casino
University of Hawaii (International Studies: Western Europe; German Language & Literature, M.A.)
Woosong University, English Instructor

Steve Homer
Northwestern University, B.S. in Journalism (Honors graduate, class of 1988)
YBM Inc. Editorial Department, Senior Writer and Editor Freelance Writer and Editor

행복한 명작 읽기 **48** Grade 5

주홍글씨
The Scarlet Letter

원작 Nathaniel Hawthorne　　**각색** Michael Robert Bradie
펴낸이 정규도　**펴낸곳** (주)다락원

초판 1쇄 발행 2006년 6월 25일　**초판 6쇄 발행** 2020년 3월 19일

책임편집 김지영, 김명진　**디자인** 손혜정, 박은진
일러스트 Julina Aleckcangra　**녹음** Michael Yancey, Christopher Hughes, Anna Paik
번역 한은숙

다락원 경기도 파주시 문발로 211
Tel (02)736-2031 (출판부: 내선 523　영업부: 내선 250~252)　Fax 02)732-2037
출판등록 1977년 9월 16일 제406-2008-000007호
Copyright © 2006, 다락원

값 7,000원 (오디오 CD 1개 포함)　ISBN 89-5995-088-2 48740

http://www.darakwon.co.kr
- 다락원 홈페이지를 방문하시면 상세한 출판정보와 함께 동영상강좌, MP3자료 등 다양한 어학 정보를 얻으실 수 있습니다